MIGHTY CHRIST

MIGHTY CHRIST

R. C. SPROUL

Christian Focus Publications

© 1995 R C Sproul
ISBN 1-85792-148-8

Published by
Christian Focus Publications Ltd.
Geanies House, Fearn, Ross-shire,
IV20 1TW, Scotland, Great Britain.

Cover design by Keith Jackson

Scripture quotations are from the New International Version,
Copyright 1973, 1978, 1984 by International Bible Society. Used
by permission of the Hodder Headline Plc group

Printed and bound in Great Britain
by The Guernsey Press Co. Ltd, Vale, Guernsey, C.I.

Contents

Contents

Introduction

IN THE LAST SUMMER OF JESUS' EARTHLY MINISTRY, BEFORE he went to Jerusalem to be executed, he and his disciples faced a severe crisis.

Sometimes, when we think about the life and ministry of Jesus, we telescope the events surrounding it, and think of him walking from town to town in Galilee, and coming back and forth out of Jerusalem, followed constantly by thronging multitudes pressing up against him, all of them wanting to hear every word that came out of his mouth.

Actually, if we look carefully at the record of the earthly ministry of Jesus, we will see that public opinion regarding Jesus was similar to the New York Stock Market; it was that volatile, it went up and down.

There were times, towards the beginning of his public ministry, when the people were clamouring with enthusiasm as they watched Jesus perform a miracle here in Cana and then in Capernaum, and so on. But then there came a point in his public ministry, where, to the best of our ability to discern the historical situation, people became disenchanted and disillusioned with what Jesus was doing.

This change in attitude towards Jesus increased after he had fed over five thousand people from only five loaves and two fish. The incident occurred near to the Sea of Galilee and we can read the details in John 6. The people, after they were fed, demanded that Jesus become their king. When he refused, and explained to them that they were following him for the wrong reasons, they became angry and left him. As these disciples left, Jesus turned to the few that remained, and asked, 'You do not want to leave too, do you?' It was Peter who replied, 'Lord, to whom shall we go? You have the words of eternal life. We believe and know that you are the Holy One of God.'

But not only were the common people in Galilee changing their attitude towards Jesus, growing consolidated opposition was taking place in Jerusalem. The religious authorities there had been outraged by the teaching of Jesus, and especially his criticisms of them. They conspired to set traps for Jesus so that they could destroy him (Mark 3:6). Also, Herod Antipas, who presided over Judea, was becoming very suspicious of what he saw as Jesus' political ambitions and he was keeping a watchful eye over Jesus' activities (Luke 9:9; 13:31).

All of these things came together and produced a climate in and around Jerusalem, and throughout the whole area of Judea, that made it unsafe for Jesus to remain there.

The portrait of Jesus in the New Testament is not that of a coward who flees from confrontations, far from it. But there were occasions where he said, 'My hour is not yet come' (John 7:6, 30; 8:20). It is as if Jesus was saying, 'I will determine the place and the time of the ultimate confrontation that I am going to have with the authorities. I am not going to go by their agenda or their timetable.'

Therefore when this time of crisis came, Jesus, with a few of his disciples, went into retreat and left Jerusalem and Judea and travelled up to the northern tip of Galilee. There, in relative seclusion from the masses, Jesus and his disciples spent a short time in a little town called Caesarea Philippi. (We shouldn't confuse Caesarea Philippi with the city on the Mediterranean coast called Caesarea that was built in honour of the emperor Caesar Augustus and had grown to become one of the largest cities in Palestine.)

Caesarea Philippi was inland, and had been rebuilt by Philip, the Tetrarch of that area, in honour not of Augustus Caesar, but of Tiberias Caesar. It was located near to Mount Hermon, near to the little springs and brooks that together fed the starting point for the River Jordan. There Jesus took his disciples aside and asked a crisis question.

It is basically that question — who is Jesus? — that we are going to be examining in the first section of six chapters. Then in the second section, also of six chapters, we will look at what the Bible says Jesus did and of some of the ways we have benefited from his work.

part one

Jesus

Who is he?

1

The Son of Man

When Jesus came to the region of Caesarea Philippi, he asked his disciples, 'Who do people say the Son of Man is?' (Matthew 16:13)

DID YOU NOTICE ANYTHING STRANGE ABOUT THE WAY JESUS put the question to his disciples? He didn't simply ask his disciples, What are they saying about me?

When Lyndon Johnson was the President of the United States, it was reported that on any occasion when being interviewed by the press, he would refer to the latest Gallup poll. He always knew, up to the minute, what the drift of public opinion was. Sometimes we are cynical about politicians because, instead of leading the people, they move in the direction in which the people are already moving!

That is not the kind of leader Jesus was. Jesus would not acquiesce with public opinion and do what others wanted. He determined his own agenda. So when he questioned the disciples about public opinion, he did not ask, 'Who do they say I am?' Instead, at the very moment Jesus is asking what other people think about him, he uses a title to identify himself to his disciples: he refers to himself as 'the Son of Man'. The way this title is used by Jesus in the New Testament has unusual connections.

Popular titles of Jesus

If you were to go through the four Gospels, or the whole New Testament for that matter, and list the numerical frequency of the titles used for Jesus, which do you suppose would be used most often?

The answer is the title, *Christ*. In fact, this title is used of Jesus so often in the New Testament that many people think that 'Christ' is part of his name. But his name would have been 'Jesus bar-Joseph'. 'Jesus' is his name; 'Christ' is a title. We shall study this title later in chapter 2, but for the present note that the word 'Christ' is the Greek equivalent to the Hebrew word for 'the Messiah'. Therefore, when the New Testament says 'Jesus Christ', it is saying 'Jesus the Messiah'.

The second most frequently used title for Jesus in the New Testament is the title 'Lord'. We shall consider the significance of this title in chapter 4. In third place, in terms of numerical frequency, is the title 'Son of Man'. It is used about 80 times. What is striking about the use of the title is this: it is the title that Jesus most frequently used to describe himself. Of all the times that this title is used of Jesus in the New Testament, only two or three times is it used by someone other than Jesus.

I find in teaching adult classes and even in theological seminary, that if I ask my students, 'Why does Jesus call himself the Son of Man?', there is a common answer. Generally the response is that the title 'Son of Man' was a humble, self-designation that Jesus used to call attention to his humanity, his identification with us as people. There is an element of truth in this answer, but it is inadequate.

The New Testament has another title for Jesus, 'Son of God'. In the history of Christianity, the church has confessed its faith that Jesus, though he is one person, has two natures, one divine and one human. Therefore, if we think that the title 'Son of God' is used in the New Testament for Jesus' divinity, it is easy to jump to the conclusion that when it uses the title, 'Son of Man', it is with reference to his humanity. But if we jump, we are going to jump into all kinds of trouble, because it simply isn't a valid conclusion. If anything, the situation is reversed.

> *What is striking about the use of the title 'Son of Man' is this: it is the title that Jesus most frequently used to describe himself.*

In the Bible, the title, 'Son of God', is ascribed to angels and also to human beings, with specific reference to people who are particularly obedient to God. This is not to say that the title 'Son of God' has no reference to the deity of Christ; it does, particularly the special way in which it is used of Jesus. But the phrase, in and of itself, often refers to creatures and doesn't necessarily indicate deity. Similarly, although the title 'Son of Man' has reference to Jesus' solidarity with humanity, there is something about the biblical use of this title which focuses on the transcendent majesty of Christ.

MIGHTY CHRIST

Daniel's vision
This phrase, 'the Son of Man', was not invented by Jesus
in the first century, but has its roots in Old Testament
literature, particularly in the book of Daniel. Daniel is a
difficult book to interpret because it is apocalyptic literature, with vivid images.

In the seventh chapter of Daniel, the prophet is de-
scribing a vision which God gave him of the inner sanc-
tum in heaven. He is transported, as it were, by the Spirit,
much as John was on the Isle of Patmos when he wrote
the book of Revelation. Daniel was given the privilege of
looking into the interior of heaven itself. In writing of
what he saw, he uses sharp crystal images to describe his
experience. If you are familiar with the book of Revelation, you will realise that it is almost verbatim recapitula-
tion of this scene in Daniel.

First of all, Daniel describes what he saw in the vision:

'As I looked,
    thrones were set in place,
        and the Ancient of Days took his seat.
His clothing was as white as snow;
        the hair of his head was white like wool.
His throne was flaming with fire,
        and its wheels were all ablaze.
A river of fire was flowing,
        coming out from before him.
Thousands upon thousands attended him;
        ten thousand times ten thousand stood before him.

> The court was seated,
> and the books were opened' (Daniel 7:9,10).

Do you get the picture? Daniel, looking into the inner court of heaven, sees someone seated on this throne of splendour who has the title, 'the Ancient of Days'. He is referring to God the Father, seated in regal splendour upon the throne, surrounded and attended by tens of thousands of angelic beings.

The scene portrayed is that of a courtroom where, with the Judge seated, the court comes to order, and the books are opened. We can imagine how breathtaking this was for the prophet: to see the future when the Ancient of Days will be seated on the throne of authority and judgment. But Daniel kept looking. And this is what he saw:

> 'In my vision at night I looked, and there before me was one like a son of man, coming with the clouds of heaven. He approached the Ancient of Days and was led into his presence. He was given authority, glory and sovereign power; all peoples, nations and men of every language worshipped him. His dominion is an everlasting dominion that will not pass away, and his kingdom is one that will never be destroyed' (verses 13, 14).

Daniel is saying, 'I looked into heaven itself, and as the court was come to order with the books opened, suddenly I saw the *Shekinah* cloud: the visible, tangible, perceivable manifestation of the blinding glory of God himself. And in this cloud, being brought in to the throne room, was One who was identified as the Son of Man. This Son of Man was brought to the immediate presence of the Ancient of Days, and presented to him. The Ancient of Days then commanded that the Son of Man be given dominion and glory and an everlasting kingdom.' What Daniel saw was the exaltation of Christ.

We are not going to examine every occurrence of this title, 'the Son of Man', in the Old and New Testaments, but essentially the title is used, not to describe a human being whose sphere of operations is the earth, but a heavenly being. It concerns One who left the presence of the Ancient of Days in heaven, became human, and at the completion of his sojourn returned to his place of origin, heaven itself, where he was given dominion, glory and a kingdom.

It is no accident that when, after his resurrection, Jesus left this world from the Mount of Olives, the biblical description is that he ascended in a cloud of glory which disappeared beyond the vision of the disciples (Acts 1:9). Luke, the author of Acts, tells us of the departure of Jesus, but he does not describe the arrival at the other end. It is that arrival which Daniel saw.

Jesus once made this statement: 'No one has ever gone into heaven except the one who came from heaven — the Son of Man' (John 3:13). In fact he frequently made reference to the fact that his place of origin was not Bethlehem. Yes, he was born in Bethlehem, but he predated his own birth. He repeatedly stressed the fact that he came from above, that he came from the Father. He descended from heaven before he ever ascended to heaven.

Two incidents in the life of Jesus

Two episodes in Jesus' ministry call attention to the significance of this title, 'Son of Man'.

On one occasion Jesus healed a crippled person. In the act of healing him he said, 'Take heart, son; your sins are forgiven' (Matthew 9:2). When the religious authorities heard this, they were furious. They thought that Jesus was just a human being making himself out to be God.

As twentieth-century people, we are accustomed to hearing ministers and priests pronounce the promise of God's forgiveness on people who repent of their sins. Jesus commissioned the church to make those utterances in his name. Therefore it doesn't offend us.

In the Jewish community of the first century, however, it was clearly understood that the only person who had the authority to forgive sins was God. Yet when Jesus ministered to the crippled man, he didn't say, 'Let me pray for you that my Father will forgive your sins.' Unilaterally he made a declaration: 'Your sins are forgiven.' That is why there was an angry response with the charge of blasphemy being brought against him.

How did Jesus respond? 'Knowing their thoughts, Jesus said, "Why do you entertain evil thoughts in your hearts? Which is easier: to say, 'Your sins are forgiven,' or to say, 'Get up and walk'? But so that you may know

that the Son of Man has authority on earth to forgive sins
... ." Then he said to the paralytic, "Get up, take your mat
and go home" ' (Matthew 9:4-6).

Jesus did this to teach them something. What was the
lesson? He performed the miracle so the onlookers would
know that he, the Son of Man, had authority to forgive
sins. That is not a statement of self-effacing humility, and
his contemporaries understood this. When they heard Jesus saying that the Son of Man had the authority to forgive sins on earth, they knew he was claiming to be divine.

The other occasion was when the disciples ate some
corn as they walked through a cornfield on a Sabbath day
(Mark 2:23-28). The Pharisees found fault with their behaviour. Jesus, in his explanation of why he had permit-
ted his disciples to eat the corn, said, 'The Sabbath was
made for man, not man for the Sabbath. So the Son of
Man is Lord even of the Sabbath.'

Listen to that with the ears of a first-century Jew, who
understood that only the Creator of the universe had lord-
ship over the Sabbath day. The Sabbath had not been es-
tablished by Moses but by God, so when Jesus said, 'the
Son of Man is Lord of the Sabbath', he was saying, 'the
Son of Man is God.'

Taking these two incidents together, we can see that
the title 'the Son of Man' bespeaks divine authority to
forgive sins and to authorise what was acceptable Sabbath behaviour. Both areas belonged exclusively to God
and so when Jesus used the title to describe himself, he
was saying that he was God.

2

Prophet and Christ

When Jesus came to the region of Caesarea Philippi, he asked his disciples, 'Who do people say the Son of Man is?'

They replied, 'Some say John the Baptist; others say Elijah; and still others, Jeremiah or one of the prophets.'

'But what about you?' he asked. 'Who do you say I am?'

Simon Peter answered, 'You are the Christ, the Son of the living God' (Matthew 16:13-16).

IN CHAPTER 1, WE CONSIDERED THE QUESTION JESUS PUT TO his disciples: 'Who do people say the Son of Man is?' We discovered that Jesus revealed his deity by using his favourite title of self-designation, 'Son of Man'. In this chapter we will consider the answer the disciples gave to the question.

As I mentioned in the Introduction, public opinion about Jesus was vacillating. Early on in his ministry people believed that he was the Messiah, but their concept of Messiah was almost entirely political. They were looking for somebody who would deliver them from the bondage of Rome. When Jesus refused to mould himself into that concept of a Messiah, the people began to wonder who he actually was.

The answer of the disciples was: 'Some say John the Baptist; others say Elijah; and still others, Jeremiah or one of the prophets.' That is a fascinating selection of answers.

Jesus and John the Baptist

Why would anybody think that Jesus was John the Baptist? How could they confuse Jesus with John? Actually, at another time, people were upset because Jesus was so different from John the Baptist:

'To what, then, can I compare the people of this generation? What are they like? They are like children sitting in the marketplace and calling out to each other: "We played the flute for you, and you did not dance; we sang a dirge, and you did not cry." For John the Baptist came neither eating bread nor drinking wine, and you say, "He has a demon." The Son of Man came eating and drinking, and you say, "Here is a glutton and a drunkard, a friend of tax collectors and 'sinners'." But wisdom is proved right by all her children' (Luke 7:31-35).

When John the Baptist came on the scene, he looked like a wild man, wearing a loincloth and eating only locusts and wild honey. He did not touch wine and did not seem to associate with any kind of fun or games. But when Jesus came on the scene, he was accused of being a drunkard and a glutton, because he attended events such as the wedding feast at Cana. So why would anyone confuse the two?

Actually they had a lot in common. Not only were they related (see Luke 1:36), but when John began his public ministry his message to the people of Israel was: 'Repent, for the kingdom of heaven is near' (Matthew 3:2). Similarly, Jesus began his earthly ministry with the message: 'Repent, for the kingdom of heaven is near' (Matthew 4:17).

It is true that by the time of this incident at Caesarea Philippi John had been executed by Herod. But for a short period of time in Israel, John the Baptist was more famous than Jesus. John was the first prophet to appear in four hundred years; he instituted radical procedures, such as the baptism of Jews; he challenged the king over his lifestyle. All of that made for controversy and resulted in his fame spreading across the countryside.

So when suddenly he disappeared from public view and the rumour spread that he had been executed, not everybody believed it. Some people were still looking for John the Baptist to re-appear and start his fabulous ministry all over again. Therefore when one appeared who preached like John, who was bold like John, who performed a prophetic ministry like John, people began to think, 'Jesus is John the Baptist come back.'

Their interest in Jesus was probably based on the last prophecy in the Old Testament, found at the close of the Book of Malachi. God promised that before the Day of the Lord came, he would send the prophet Elijah back to this earth. Even to this day, Jewish people leave an empty chair at the table during the celebration of the Passover in case Elijah comes. In Jesus' day there was a great deal of excitement concerning the arrival of the kingdom of God. People said, 'If Jesus isn't the Messiah, then maybe he's the forerunner of the Messiah.'

The people realised that Jesus was a prophet

There is no need for a detailed examination of the possible reasons why people would have speculated about these personages. But notice they all have something in common: the public perception that Jesus was a prophet. This was not a small designation. To be a prophet in Israel was not to be a fortune-teller, an astrologer or a crystal-ball gazer. In Jewish theology, a prophet was singularly endowed and anointed by God to speak the very word of God to people.

When a prophet gave an oracle, as the Spirit of God came upon him, he didn't say, 'In my considered judgment' or 'In my opinion' or 'I think this or I think that'. He prefaced his announcements with the words: 'This is what the Lord says'. The Jews perceived that a prophet was one whose message had its origin ultimately in God, that the prophet was an agent of divine revelation.

In Israel, there were two offices with religious significance: the priest and the prophet. Those who held these offices had many things in common: they were anointed by God, they were set apart by God, they were gifted by God, and they functioned as mediators.

When we think of mediators today we picture someone standing between hostile forces, like labour and management. But a mediator in the classical sense was simply a go-between, someone who stands in the middle between two parties, and speaks for one or other of those parties.

The role of the priest was to speak to God on behalf of the people. The people would ask their priest to pray for them, and he would intercede with God. But the opposite was the case with the prophet. The prophet spoke to the people for God. He was God's spokesman.

One of the ironies of history is that there are many people today who are not persuaded that Jesus was divine. But they still attempt to honour him by suggesting with great facility, 'Jesus was a wonderful prophet.' But what they mean is that they have respect for the wisdom of Jesus. They are certainly not using the word 'prophet' in the biblical sense.

> What makes Jesus different from every other prophet in biblical history is that he is a prophet *par excellence*.

What makes Jesus different from every other prophet in biblical history is that he is a prophet *par excellence*. He is not first among equals, but is in a class by himself. Jesus as a prophet not only pronounced the word of God, but declared that he himself was the living and incarnate word of God. In other words: Jesus not only delivered the word of God, he was the word of God.

All other prophets uttered prophecies and the content of their prophecy was the promised Redeemer of Israel. But Jesus was himself both the subject and the object of his prophecy. In simple language, this means that the central message of the prophetic teaching of Jesus Christ, was Jesus Christ. That's why people today cannot really believe that he was a prophet, in the biblical sense of the word, without believing that he is the Son of God.

Jesus is the Christ

Jesus did not make much comment on this public opinion survey. Instead, he turned to his friends who were on retreat with him, looked them in the face and said, 'Who do you say that I am? It is interesting to hear what the public opinion is; it is interesting to know the various theories; but I want to know what you think.' No doubt Jesus' gaze went from one face to another, among his closest friends.

The spokesman for the disciples was Simon, the big fisherman. Simon answered this question with words which have been described as the first creed of historic Christianity. When Jesus said to them, 'But what about you? Who do you say I am?' Simon Peter answered, 'You are the Christ, the Son of the living God.'

Simon gives a dual answer. First he states the very thing that the multitudes had abandoned, the concept that they had earlier embraced and then despaired of when Jesus wouldn't fit their expectations as the promised Messiah; Peter says, 'You are the Christ!' Secondly, Jesus having referred to himself as the Son of Man in his question, Peter in his answer says that Jesus is the Son of the Living God.

I have close friends who are practising Jews. We often sit down and discuss the various aspects of our religion. We have warm and friendly talks about ethics and the principal concerns of human dignity.

Yet all the time we know that there is a critical point of difference which we cannot get past: I believe that the Messiah has come and they do not. And that is the pivotal issue in the history of Judaeo-Christianity: Is Jesus of Nazareth the One whom God had promised to send to deliver his people?

Part of the reason why people do not agree as to whether Jesus was the Christ or not, is because this very concept is so multifaceted, so deep and profound.

The word 'Christ' comes over into English from the Greek word *christos* and the word *christos* is the Greek equivalent of the Hebrew *messiach*, which comes over in English as 'Messiah'. Literally the word *christos* means 'anointed one'.

In the Old Testament there were lots of christs, although not in the ultimate sense. Anyone who was anointed by God for a vocation was an 'anointed one'. When the priest, the prophet or the king was anointed, he was *christos* in the general sense. As the promises of God became clearer, God began to say that, at some future point in history, he would send One who would be ultimately and singularly anointed.

The Reformers summarised the concept of Messiah by saying it had at least three elements. He would be *a prophet*, because God said that in the future he would send a prophet like Moses (Deuteronomy 18:15); *a king*, because the Messiah was to be from the line of David, and would inherit an everlasting kingdom (Isaiah 9:7); *a priest*, for the Messiah was to be a high priest after the order of Melchisedek (Psalm 110:4).

The role of the Messiah which captured the people's imagination was his being a king. The most difficult to appreciate was his priestly work. Just as the Old Testament prophet was the subject of prophecy but not the object of prophecy, so the Old Testament priest was the subject of sacrifice but never the object of sacrifice. But the Messiah, as a High Priest after the order of Melchisedek, was not only the one who offered the supreme sacrifice to God, but was himself the sacrifice of God. The Messiah-priest was both subject and object of priesthood.

These are only some of the strands which come together in any proper understanding of the Messiah. Undoubtedly it was difficult to understand. What then did Jesus say to Peter in response to his answer? Did he look at him and say, 'Simon, that's a profoundly interesting theological speculation.' Or did he say, 'Simon, you're just guessing, like the rest of the people were guessing when I fed the multitude.' That's not what he said. He looked at Simon and pronounced a divine benediction on him: 'Blessed are you, Simon son of Jonah, for this was not revealed to you by man, but by my Father in heaven.'

At first glance, Jesus' statement is a little strange. We might think that, with all the available evidence and the clear fulfilment of prophecy, it would not require any divine revelation to recognise the identity of Jesus. But Jesus made his appearance at a time when the hearts of the people were hardened. They couldn't hear the word of God when it was spoken to them. They couldn't recognise the Son of God when he was right before their very eyes. But God took the scales from Peter's eyes and he recognised that Jesus was the Messiah!

Jesus acknowledged to the disciples that he was the Christ. What he said next though was very surprising. He and the disciples were speaking among themselves, in retreat and isolation from the pressing multitudes. Jesus instructed the disciples, however, that they should tell no one that he was the Christ. Why? Because Israel was still not ready for the full understanding of the Messiah. What the people could not understand was the priestly element. The Messiah was not only to be a king, he had also to be the Suffering Servant of Israel.

In the next chapter we are going to see that, blessed as Peter was, as true as his confession was, even he at this point didn't understand that the Messiah-King, the Messiah-Prophet, had also to be a Messiah-Priest who would suffer.

3

The Mystery of the Messiah

From that time on Jesus began to explain to his disciples that he must go to Jerusalem and suffer many things at the hands of the elders, chief priests and teachers of the law, and that he must be killed and on the third day be raised to life.

Peter took him aside and began to rebuke him. 'Never, Lord!' he said. 'This shall never happen to you!'

Jesus turned and said to Peter, 'Get behind me, Satan! You are a stumbling-block to me; you do not have in mind the things of God, but the things of men' (Matthew 16:21-23).

I REMEMBER A FEW YEARS AGO WATCHING BURT REYNOLDS being interviewed on a television talk-show. In the course of the interview, the host asked him what it was like to have such a macho image and so on. The discussion then broadened out to include a consideration of the whole perception in our culture of what it means to be masculine. At a crucial point in that discussion, the host asked Burt Reynolds, 'Burt, at what point in a young man's development can he really say that he is a man?' Burt replied, 'A boy becomes a man when his father tells him that he is a man.'

I remember when I heard that comment that chills went up and down my spine. As a male I related to that, because all of us as men want the approval and the affirmation of other men whom we admire and respect — a father, a teacher, a coach.

Can you imagine how Simon bar-Jonah felt when, after he uttered his confession of faith, Jesus himself looked at him and said, 'You are the rock.' It is one thing to receive a compliment from a student or from a peer, but to have the Lord God incarnate look you in the eye and say, 'You are a rock' — what would that mean to any man who has ever wrestled with his manhood in the history of this planet?

The irony is that Peter's opportunity to bask in the glory of that compliment was short-lived. Within a very short space of time, Jesus not only paid Simon one of the highest compliments he ever paid a human being, he also rebuked him with the most scathing criticism he ever offered to an individual during his earthly ministry. What caused this change in such a short period of time?

Peter misunderstands the role of Jesus
Look again at the narrative of the Caesarea Philippi confession. Jesus warned his disciples not to tell anyone that he was the Christ. Then Matthew tells us:

> 'From that time on Jesus began to explain to his disciples that he must go to Jerusalem and suffer many things at the hands of the elders, chief priests and teachers of the law and that he must be killed and on the third day be raised to life.'

Now, verse 22 of the 16th chapter reads like this: 'Peter took him aside ...' — now isn't that one for the books?

Jesus tells his disciples that he must go to Jerusalem where he would be delivered over to the hands of his enemies, the very ones from whom they were hiding, up there in Caesarea Philippi. Jesus was going to walk right into their headquarters. He was going to be killed.

When the disciples heard that, they were flabbergasted. Simon Peter nudged Jesus, saying, 'We have to talk!' He took Jesus aside and began to rebuke and admonish his Master. All of a sudden the impetuous one lived up to his image, didn't he? Simon, now that he was the rock, understood that the student is above the master, the servant is above the lord; he was now going to give proper counsel to Jesus and correct Jesus' faulty theology. He said to Jesus, with emphasis: 'Never, Lord! This shall never happen to you!'

I wonder what Jesus was thinking. Here was Peter, called to be an apostle, an agent of revelation, emphatically uttering a future prediction — 'This will never happen to you!' But it did happen. Peter was wrong.

Jesus turned and said to Peter, 'Get behind me, Satan! You are a stumbling-block to me; you do not have in mind the things of God, but the things of men.' Isn't this incredible? Just a short time before this, Jesus had said to Peter, 'You are the rock and on this rock I am going to build my church and the gates of hell will not prevail against it.' Now he looked at Simon and said, 'Get behind me, Satan.'

Some would interpret this passage as indicating that, at this weak moment in Peter's experience, he was possessed by Satan and, against his will and outwith his control, these words came out of his mouth. They say that it was not really Simon Peter who was speaking but Satan who had taken control of Simon. That is not only bad theology, it is bad exegesis.

It may be that Satan incited Peter by suggesting the

idea. But remember when Jesus was in the desert for forty days tempted by Satan. After he had vanquished Satan on that occasion, we read these words in the record: 'the devil ... left him until an opportune time' (Luke 4:13). There is the foreboding sense that the devil was going to attack Jesus later on in his earthly ministry.

At the heart of Satan's attempted seduction of Jesus was his attempt to offer Jesus a crown without pain, a kingdom without suffering, a Messianic vocation without death. Jesus said 'No'. But here it comes

> The scandal of the New Testament was that the Messiah, the King, would suffer.

again, right after this magnificent confession of faith. When Peter said 'Never' to the intention of Jesus to suffer, it was the same message that Satan had suggested to Jesus in the desert.

Peter the rock had now become Satan. From stone to stumbling-block! From Rock of Gibraltar to a tripping stone! Jesus pointed out why Peter had become this: 'you do not have in mind the things of God, but the things of men.' Earlier he had blessed Simon as the recipient of divine revelation. Now he says that Peter was back on the human level, following the way of the flesh.

The scandal of the New Testament was that the Messiah, the King, would suffer. Further illustration of this is found in the fifth chapter of the Book of Revelation where John records how God gave him the privilege of looking into heaven and describes the scene: 'Then I saw in the right hand of him who sat on the throne a scroll with writing on both sides and sealed with seven seals' (verse 1). This reminds us of the judgment scene which Daniel recorded, that we thought about in Chapter 1. At the very end of that scene we saw that the court was convened and the books were opened. The focal point of this vision is a scroll (or book) at the last judgment.

John continues in verse 2: 'I saw a mighty angel proclaiming in a loud voice, "Who is worthy to break the seals and open the scroll?" ' Do you get the picture? The scroll contains the secrets of life, the mysteries of the ages, the plan of redemption. To be sealed with seven seals in Jewish imagery means that something is sealed in such a way that no mortal can pry it open; no one can peer into its contents.

Have you read the story of the bow of Ulysses? His wife, Penelope, had been besieged by suitors demanding that she set a date to marry one of them. She said, 'Whoever can bend the bow of Ulysses, I will marry.' All the strongest men in the empire came and tried to bend the bow, but they couldn't.

At this very time Ulysses made his way back home and came into his own palace disguised as a beggar. Finally the moment came in the banquet hall when this mendicant stooped over and approached the massive bow. When he came near the bow all who witnessed it began laughing. But he grabbed the bow and bent it. His hood fell off and everyone knew that Ulysses had returned.

In heaven the myriads of the angelic host all turn their

attention to see who is going to open the scroll. Listen to what John says: 'But no-one in heaven or on earth or under the earth could open the scroll or even look inside' (verse 3). The angels waited and waited; but no one stepped forward to break the seals and open the book. John wept. He was so disappointed, he broke into tears. He had thought he was going to be able to look into the secret things of God.

Then one of the elders said to him, 'Do not weep! See, the Lion of the tribe of Judah, the Root of David, has triumphed. He is able to open the scroll and its seven seals.'

In the mid-1960s, I was in graduate school in Holland. During January 1965 the news came that Great Britain's greatest hero of the twentieth century, Sir Winston Churchill, had died. London was preparing for one of the most magnificent funerals in the history of the world, the way that only the British can do it. Some student friends and I decided to go to London to pay our respects to Sir Winston.

We went to the funeral. A million people jammed the streets between St Paul's Cathedral and Westminster Abbey. As I stood on the pavement, many of the world's dignitaries marched past, right in front of my eyes. I saw Charles de Gaulle, King Constantine, Earl Warren, Dwight Eisenhower and Queen Elizabeth II.

Then there came this little man, with great regal bearing, military ribbons adorning his chest. He was announced as His Imperial Majesty the Lion of Judah, the Emperor of Ethiopia, Haile Selassie. I watched him, and thought, 'What a magnificent man this is who defied

European powers during World War II and who created the most stable government in Africa of his generation!' And I thought he was worthy of so many titles. But there is one title he did not deserve: he was not the Lion of Judah. That title belongs to the Messiah.

The lion is king of the beasts, reigning over his domain in the forest. In Jewish history, the lion was the symbol of the Davidic kingdom. David and Solomon were of the tribe of Judah. The coming Messiah would be from the line of Judah and would be the Lion of Judah. The Lion of Judah, the Root of David had overcome so as to open the scroll and the seven seals.

So John looks up waiting for the appearance of a lion. But instead of a lion, something else comes:

'Then I saw a Lamb, looking as if it had been slain, standing in the centre of the throne, encircled by the four living creatures and the elders. He had seven horns and seven eyes, which are the seven spirits of God sent out into all the earth. He came and took the scroll from the right hand of him who sat on the throne. And when he had taken it, the four living creatures and the twenty-four elders fell down before the Lamb. Each one had a harp and they were holding golden bowls full of incense, which are the prayers of the saints. And they sang a new song:

"You are worthy to take the scroll
    and to open its seals,

because you were slain,
   and with your blood you
      purchased men for God
from every tribe and language
   and people and nation.
You have made them to be
   a kingdom and priests to serve our God,
   and they will reign on the earth."

Then I looked and heard the voice of many angels,
numbering thousands upon thousands, and ten
thousand times ten thousand. They encircled the
throne and the living creatures and the elders. In a
loud voice they sang:

"Worthy is the Lamb, who was slain,
to receive power and wealth and
   wisdom and strength
and honour and glory and praise!"

Then I heard every creature in heaven and on earth
and under the earth and on the sea, and all that is in
them, singing:

"To him who sits on the throne
   and to the Lamb
be praise and honour and glory and power,
for ever and ever!"

THE MYSTERY OF THE MESSIAH

The four living creatures said, "Amen", and the
elders fell down and worshipped (5:6-14).'

Has there ever been any anthem in the history of the
church more stirring to the soul, forcing us to our feet the
moment we hear its opening strains, as the Hallelujah Cho-
rus? It is Handel's musical rendition of this scene in the
heavenly court, when a lion is introduced, but who ap-
pears as a lamb who was slain.

That's the mystery of the Messiah which was misunderstood by the people in general, and not only by them
but also by Simon Peter at Caesarea Philippi. They did
not believe that the Messiah could also be the Servant,
that the King could also be killed. Only after Jesus was
raised from the dead did the early church understand for
the first time the classic description of the Messiah as the
Suffering Servant of Israel, predicted in Isaiah 53. It was
this passage which Philip explained to the Ethiopian eu-
nuch (Acts 8:32-35). Anyone who has been a Christian
for a short time is familiar with that chapter. It is so rich,
so astonishing, yet it was written hundreds of years before Jesus was born.

Jesus was the Lion who rendered himself as a guilt
offering (Isaiah 53:10). That's what it took to be the Messiah. That's what Peter failed to understand. But later,
after his King was crucified on Calvary, he did understand what he had confessed at Caesarea Philippi: 'You
are the Christ, the Son of the Living God.'

4

Jesus is Lord

'Your attitude should be the same as that of Christ Jesus:
    Who, being in very nature God,
        did not consider equality with God
            something to be grasped,
    but made himself nothing,
        taking the very nature of a servant,
        being made in human likeness.
    And being found in appearance as a man,
        he humbled himself
        and became obedient to death –
            even death on a cross!
    Therefore God exalted him to the highest place
        and gave him the name that is above every name,
    that at the name of Jesus every knee should bow,
        in heaven and on earth and under the earth,
    and every tongue confess that Jesus Christ is Lord,
        to the glory of God the Father.'

IN OUR EXAMINATION SO FAR OF WHAT WAS SAID IN THE BRIEF exchange between Jesus and Peter during their retreat at Caesarea Philippi, we have identified several important titles for Jesus: the Son of Man, the Christ, the Son of the Living God. We have also seen that public opinion regarded Jesus as a prophet.

In this chapter we focus on another title that is applied to Jesus by Peter during their discussion: the title, 'Lord'.

Remember the words that Peter used when he took Jesus aside and began to admonish and rebuke him. Peter said: 'Never, Lord! This shall never happen to you!' Here is the disciple rebuking the very person whom he is addressing as 'Lord'.

In the first chapter we noted that the title 'Lord' is the second most used title for Jesus in the New Testament. In fact it has been said that the creed of the early church was simply this: Jesus is Lord.

A test of loyalty
One of the great crises that faced the early Christian community involved its relationship to the civil authorities, particularly to the Roman government. We can read in church history the story of the martyrdom of the saints under the persecutions of Nero and later emperors of Rome.

That horrible slaughter of believers lasted for several centuries. The Christians, by order of Nero, were coated in pitch and then set on fire, to become human torches to illumine the gardens of Nero at night. Other Christians had to deal with lions in the arena in the Circus Maximus.

What precipitated all of that was the rise of the emperor-worship cult in Rome. As an oath of loyalty, every citizen in the Roman empire had to recite a brief formula: *Caesar kurios*, which means, 'Caesar is lord'.

The Christians response was, 'We will honour the civil magistrates; we will pay our tithes and our tributes to Caesar. We will do all we can to be model citizens of Rome. But one thing we cannot say, privately or publicly, are those two words: *Caesar kurios*, because to do so would be to commit cosmic treason, because our Lord, our *kurios*, is Christ.'

The bishop of Smyrna, Polycarp, at the age of eighty-six, was charged with treason because he refused to recite the oath to Caesar. The prosecutors of the Roman state did not want to harm him. He was respected, he was venerable, he got along well with the authorities.

Polycarp was brought into the arena before thousands of spectators, but even up to the last moments the state officials wanted to spare him from execution. They gave him one last opportunity. All Polycarp had to say was 'Caesar is lord' and 'Away with the atheists!' (It is one of the ironies of history that the Christians were charged with atheism because they wouldn't worship the emperor, and because they didn't follow the cultic practices associated with the gods and goddesses of Rome.)

> The bishop of Smyrna, Polycarp, at the age of eighty-six, was charged with treason because he refused to recite the oath to Caesar.

Polycarp, in a benign way, smiled and said, 'If that's all that you want me to say, I can say that.' He looked at the stands, where were seated the representatives of the Roman state and the pagan religions, and said, 'Away with the atheists!' Not what the state had in mind! And then Polycarp said, 'Eighty-six years have I been faithful to my Lord, and for eighty-six years he has been merciful and gracious to me. How can I now deny him? *Iesus ho kurios*.' He was summarily executed. Yet the blood of the martyrs was the seed of the church.

In this regard, there is a statement by Paul in one of his letters to the church in Corinth which is perhaps difficult for us to understand. He said that no one can say 'Jesus is Lord' except by the Holy Spirit (1 Corinthians 12:3). The problem is that Jesus himself talks about those who make an insincere profession of faith. He said, 'These people honour me with their lips, but their hearts are far from me' (Matthew 15:8). He even said:

> 'Not everyone who says to me, "Lord, Lord," will
> enter the kingdom of heaven, but only he who does
> the will of my Father who is in heaven. Many will
> say to me on that day, "Lord, Lord, did we not proph-
> esy in your name, and in your name drive out de-
> mons and perform many miracles?" Then I will tell
> them plainly, "I never knew you. Away from me, you
> evildoers!" ' (Matthew 7:21-23).

Do you see the difficulty in harmonising those texts?
On the one hand Paul says that no one can even say 'Jesus
is Lord' except by the Holy Spirit. On the other hand,
however, there is the admonition and warning from Jesus
about those who say it glibly without actually meaning it.

In order to resolve those texts we have to understand
that Paul's statement is elliptical, that is, there is something tacitly understood which is not spelled out. It could
be said this way: no one can say 'Jesus is Lord' *and mean
it*, except by the Holy Spirit.

Different uses of 'Lord' in the New Testament
The title, 'Lord', which is from the Greek, *kurios*, has
three meanings attached to it in the New Testament and
these are more or less in an ascending order of weightiness.

First, there was the common use of the word, simply as a polite form of address, similar to calling somebody in our own day, 'Sir', or 'Mister'. In the Gospels, strangers, when speaking to Jesus, as a matter of course address him as 'Lord'. This did not mean that they recognised his deity.

A second usage of the term 'Lord' is similar to what happens in Britain. When someone is elevated to the peerage the word 'Lord' is put in front of his name. This is a formal title of respect and dignity. In the New Testament world, this second usage was applied to a slave-owner. A person who was wealthy enough to purchase slaves was called a *kurios*, or a lord. Usually, when it is used in this sense in the New Testament, it is translated by the word, 'Master'.

The significance of this is that a slave (*doulos*) was not the same as a hired servant. Rather, he was purchased and became the possession of the lord. We can see that language sprinkled throughout the New Testament. Paul, for example, loved to introduce himself in his letters to the early churches by saying, 'Paul, a *doulos* of the Lord Jesus.' He reminds Christians that they are not their own, but have been bought, and are now the possession of their *kurios*, Jesus.

But these are the lower order meanings of the word *kurios* in the New Testament. When we come to the third level of usage we are not simply taking another step of equal proportion, rather we are making a quantum leap. This is the supreme title of dignity, of respect, and of authority.

MIGHTY CHRIST

A divine title

To understand the significance of the title 'Lord', we need to survey its use in both the Old and New Testaments. In the Old Testament, the sacred name of God was 'Yahweh' ('LORD' in most Bible versions). In the Ten Commandments, the people of Israel were warned against abusing or misusing God's name. The Jewish people became very scrupulous about guarding themselves, lest they be found guilty of blasphemy. To do so, they used the technique known as 'periphrasis'.

In other words, the Jews devised different titles which became substitutes for the name *Yahweh*. The supreme title of substitution was *Adonai* ('Lord' in most Bible versions), meaning, the one who is absolutely sovereign. The Jews also used the word *Melech,* which means king, but that was a lesser title. *Adonai* is the one who is sovereign over the kings of the world.

The Old Testament text which is most frequently quoted or alluded to by the New Testament writers is Psalm 110. Psalm 110 begins like this: 'The LORD says to my Lord: Sit at my right hand.' What David, the author, wrote was: 'Yahweh says to my Adonai.' God is having a conversation with someone whom David is addressing as Adonai. And Adonai is God's title! The New Testament picks up on that theme and tells us that Jesus is, at the same time, the son of David and the Lord of David (Matthew 22:41-46). David's Son was David's Adonai. It is that supreme title, the equivalent of Adonai, the title reserved for God himself, which is bestowed upon Jesus in the New Testament.

So far, in the book, we have looked at several names of Jesus. But what was God's favourite name for Jesus?

The answer to that question is found in Philippians 2:5-11. This well-known passage is frequently called a *Kenotic Hymn*:

'Your attitude should be the same as that of Christ Jesus:
   Who, being in very nature God,
      did not consider equality with God
        something to be grasped,
   but made himself nothing,
      taking the very nature of a servant,
      being made in human likeness.
  And being found in appearance as a man,
      he humbled himself
      and became obedient to death –
        even death on a cross!
  Therefore God exalted him to the highest place
    and gave him the name that is above every name,
  that at the name of Jesus every knee should bow,
      in heaven and on earth and under the earth,
  and every tongue confess that Jesus Christ is Lord,
      to the glory of God the Father.'

If we read the hymn too quickly we may jump to the conclusion that the 'name that is above every name', is 'Jesus'. But in fact 'Jesus' was a common name, the Greek equivalent of Joshua. It is not the name 'Jesus' which is exalted above every name, it is the title, *kurios*.

MIGHTY CHRIST

Jesus is not only *kurios*, Lord, but he is *kurios kurion*, which means Lord of lords. He is the one to whom all sovereignty in the entire universe has been given by the Father. That is the name by which we express our allegiance, our reverence and our adoration of Jesus.

5

The Glory of God

I saw none of the other apostles –
only James, the Lord's brother.
(Galatians 1:19)

James, a servant of God
and of the Lord Jesus Christ,
To the twelve tribes scattered among the nations
(James 1:1)

My brothers, as believers in our glorious
Lord Jesus Christ, don't show favouritism.
(James 2:1)

So far in our study of the titles of Jesus, we have considered how his contemporaries estimated him, how his disciples regarded him, how he viewed himself, and how God honoured him.

But there remains one more testimony from those who knew Jesus. This testimony comes from someone who perhaps knew Jesus more closely than any other human, namely, Jesus' own brother, James.

Recently I have been involved as editor-in-chief of *The New Geneva Study Bible*. In addition to being the general editor, the other responsibility I have had is to create the notes for the Epistle of James.

Have you ever studied a familiar passage of the Bible, when suddenly you see something in the text that you have never seen before? It is a striking discovery and you wonder how you could have missed it. I had that kind of experience as I studied the letter of James.

James 2:1 reads as follows: 'My brothers, as believers in our glorious Lord Jesus Christ, don't show favouritism.' The theme James is going to develop is that of preferential treatment: Because God is not a respecter of persons, neither should we be. Since that is the theme, we can easily fail to appreciate the words that James writes in verse one.

The phrase that we can miss without catching its massive significance is *our glorious Lord Jesus Christ*. You may have a different translation of the New Testament, where the phrase is rendered a little differently. The reason is that there is an unusual linguistic construction in this sentence. Basically, this sentence is saying that Jesus is the Glory of God.

Although there were several people called James in the New Testament community, there is a high degree of probability that this James is the one who became the leader of the Jerusalem church, presided at the Council of Jerusalem (recorded in Acts 15) and whom Paul calls the brother of Jesus (Galatians 1:19). James was a younger brother of Jesus, who watched his brother working in the carpenter's shop of Joseph, and shared the same mother, Mary. He watched the development of his older brother, but did not believe in the deity of Jesus prior to the resurrection.

It is probable that James had a sudden conversion when the risen Jesus appeared to him (1 Corinthians 15:7). James knew his brother had died and had been buried. But when he saw his brother alive again, he was converted, and became a pillar of the early Christian community.

James had a title bestowed upon him by his contemporaries. He was called James the Just, or James the Righteous One, because he exhibited extraordinary qualities of righteousness and of virtue. It was said of him that he spent so much time praying that his knees developed calluses so thick that they resembled the knees of a camel.

Obviously all the books of the New Testament are inspired by the Holy Spirit and have nothing less than the authority of God behind them. In this regard it does not matter whether the human authors were apostles or in the apostolic entourage, because the ultimate author of the Scripture is the Holy Spirit. But it is surely interesting that the book of James is the viewpoint of a man who was the blood brother of Jesus.

> James, the brother of Jesus, does not hesitate to call his own brother *kurios*, Lord.

What is glory?

James, as a Jew, understood that 'glory' was a word pregnant with meaning. It did not have the cheap association among the Jews that it now has in our culture. When a basketball player is trying to win a championship, he may say, 'I am going for glory.' When a football player wins the Superbowl, some say, 'He covered himself with glory.' That's a superficial understanding of glory.

The word for 'glory' in Greek comes from the word *doxe*, from which we get the word 'doxology'. In Hebrew it is the word *kabhodh* (pronounced *kavoth*) which literally means 'heaviness' or 'weightiness', that which has pre-eminent substance. When the Bible speaks of the glory of God, it is not saying that God weighs so many tons; rather it is saying that there is a weight of significance or importance that is uniquely found in his very being. We can distinguish between the internal glory of God (the glory of what he is, in and of himself) and the outward manifestation of that glory.

When God revealed his glory in the Old Testament, he did it through a cloud that was called a *Shekinah*. No-one is sure what it looked like, but it would be distinguished from other clouds by its blazing refulgence. Something was happening with light that was extraordinary.

The function of light

A few years ago I was occupied pursuing a layman's understanding of astrophysics and astronomy. The more I read of contemporary scientific investigations into the nature and behavioural patterns of light, the more I had the sense of approaching something on the edge of the mystical. Light is an incredible thing.

What colour is a lemon? You may reply, A lemon is yellow. No, it isn't. A lemon is black. Colour is a secondary quality which is not inherent in substances. Why does a lemon look yellow to us? Because of its chemical make-up. The light that travels towards the lemon is carrying within itself all the rich and intense hues and colours of the spectrum, as seen in the rainbow. When the light hits the lemon, many of the colours that are inherent in light are absorbed by the lemon. The lemon divides and refracts the light coming to it, and gives us yellow, one of the colours of the rainbow.

On a sunny day, when there are a few scattered clouds in the sky, sometimes we see a light show in the heavens. There is a kind of iridescence around the edges of the clouds because the light strikes them in such a way as to diffuse the rays of the sun. In Old Testament days, when God manifested his glory, he used a cloud to put on a refracted display of light which was so unique and dazzling that people were overwhelmed even if they only caught a glimpse of it. And that glory became the outward sign of the immediate presence of God.

James, the brother of Jesus, does not hesitate to call his own brother *kurios*, Lord (1:1). In the same verse he confesses his faith that his brother is *Christos*, the Christ (1:1). But here in 2:1 he says, 'My brother is the living incarnation of the glory of God. He is the Shekinah.'

But it wasn't always clear. At Christmas time, it is traditional to emphasise the lowly circumstances of Jesus' entrance into this world in stark contrast to the biblical description of his second advent. The return of Jesus will be a coming on clouds of glory, on the Shekinah cloud. It will be a brilliant manifestation of the weightiness of his significance, and no one will miss it.

But the first time he came, it was virtually incognito.

A visit to Bethlehem
A few years ago I had the opportunity to go to Palestine and I went on tours to the sacred sites.

One trip was to Bethlehem, to visit the church built on the traditional spot where the manger was. The guide gave his rehearsed speech which was interesting, but I got a little tired, left the group and went outside.

I wandered away from the church and went over to an old stone wall. It was a bright sunny day and, from the vantage point of the wall, I could look out over the seemingly unending plain called the Fields of Bethlehem. It was on those plains that the shepherds tended the flocks.

As I sat there, I began to let my imagination roam freely. I thought, 'Imagine what it was like that night when, like hundreds of nights before, the shepherds were performing the tedious task of night sentries. With absolutely no warning, the sky suddenly became brighter than noon.'

We read in Luke 2:8-10 (I like the King James rendering): 'And there were in the same country shepherds abiding in the field, keeping watch over their flock by night. And, lo, the angel of the Lord came upon them, and the glory of the Lord shone round about them: and they were sore afraid. And the angel said unto them, Fear not: for, behold, I bring you good tidings of great joy, which shall be to all people.'

All was quiet and then suddenly an angel appeared, and accompanying the angel was this overwhelming display of the glory of God, shining, radiating, penetrating the air all around them. Their immediate response was abject terror.

I thought, 'What would happen to my heart if I were sitting out there in the darkness and all of a sudden the glory of God shone around about me and I was face to face with an angel?' I would be terrified.

But the words of the angel calmed them. 'And the angel said unto them, Fear not: for, behold, I bring you good tidings of great joy, which shall be to all people. For unto you is born this day in the city of David a Saviour, which is Christ the Lord. And this shall be a sign unto you; Ye shall find the babe wrapped in swaddling clothes, lying in a manger' (Luke 2:10-12).

Then suddenly there appeared with the angel a multitude of the heavenly host. Not just one angel, but myriads of angels, singing, praising God. The theme of their song was 'Glory to God in the highest.'

But in the incarnation, for the most part, the refulgent, dazzling glory of the being of God was concealed, hidden behind the veil of Jesus' humanity. And as we have seen already, this is something that Jesus did willingly. He downplayed his glory and his dignity by taking upon himself the outward display of servanthood. In theology this is described as the humiliation of Jesus. He concealed his glory, and so the normal portrait of Jesus in the Bible is one of humility and of hiddenness.

But there were moments when it seemed as though the veil of his humanity could not conceal the glory, and it burst out.

The Transfiguration of Jesus

Six days after the conclusion of the episode at Caesarea Philippi, Jesus took three of his disciples (the inner circle: Peter, James and John) and led them up a high mountain. Caesarea Philippi was very near Mount Hermon which is presumably the mountain referred to.

There Jesus was transfigured: his face shone like the sun and his garments became as white as light. Whatever colour had been in the garments of Jesus vanished. Now there was the purity of the manifestation of light. No refraction; no absorption. Pure, unvarnished light. His face began to glow, radiating a light of its own, as intense as the light of the sun itself, such that no human being could gaze upon it without destroying his own eyes. This description defies human comprehension and it is simply called the Transfiguration.

In that rare moment of Transfiguration, God gave these three disciples the ability to see into another dimension. It wasn't an hallucination of glory, rather they were able to see the reality that had been concealed until then. They saw the unveiled glory of Christ.

Is it any wonder that when John wrote his Gospel years later, he began by saying that the Word of God was the light of men (John 1:4,5). At the close of the prologue, he says, 'The Word became flesh and made his dwelling among us. We have seen his glory, the glory of the One and Only, who came from the Father, full of grace and truth' (John 1:14).

Jesus doesn't merely reflect the glory of God; he is the Glory of God.

6

Bishop of Our Souls

For you were like sheep going astray, but now you have returned to the Shepherd and Overseer (or Bishop) of your souls (1 Peter 2:25).

Do you recall any occasion when you were desperately trying to get someone's attention? I once had such a frustrating experience.

My wife had been with me for two weeks as I travelled across America giving lectures. We were finally scheduled to return home from North Carolina, and we arrived at the railway station in good time for our departure. When the moment came for the train to pull into the station, the station master announced that this train was a particularly long one and therefore it would make two stops. We were told that we would board the train on the second stop and were directed to the relevant platform.

Vesta and I stood there, along with one other person, an attractive young college student. The conductor came along, stopped at the young lady, looked at her ticket, then picked up her baggage and led her down the platform. While he was doing this, I was standing there with our tickets, trying desperately to get his attention to see if he wanted to look at them, but he had no eyes for me whatsoever.

Vesta and I walked to the edge of the platform. But the train didn't stop, it went right past us and pulled out of the station. I knew that there wasn't another train for twenty-four hours. I didn't know what to do. I wanted to scream, I wanted to run down the track and say, 'Stop this train!' But the conductor had no eyes for me. He didn't see us.

Apparently, he wasn't watching closely. There was something wrong with his vision, and he made the decision to pull out without us.

That frustrating experience was an example of what happens when people don't look at us carefully, and don't look after us closely.

The whole business of looking at things carefully is at the very heart of scientific enterprise.

In 1990 the United States of America put the most expensive telescope ever made into outer space. The first estimate of the cost of the Hubble Telescope was $1.5 billion, a revised estimate took that to over $2 billion. The instrument has the capacity to increase our vision of outer space by a factor of 350 times. We can look more crisply and closely at distant objects and obtain a greater insight into the universe in which we live.

We also have sophisticated microscopes by which we can look at small things, probing what is invisible to the naked eye. There is a big difference between a telescope and a microscope, but they have this in common: the root word, 'scope' which comes from the Greek word *scopis*, meaning 'looking or seeing'.

The name Episcopalian comes from the Greek word

episkopis. Notice, it is the same word 'scope' with a prefix added to it. The word *episkopis* occurs frequently in the New Testament and is translated by the English term 'bishop'. The reason why Episcopalians are so called is because the Episcopal church is a denomination which is organised and run by bishops.

In this chapter we are going to take a close look at the meaning of the term *episkopis*. We have already seen that the root of it, *skopis*, refers to something that we 'look through' or 'look at'. The prefix *epi*, only adds emphasis to the word, and causes it to mean an 'intense scope'. So, in its simplest meaning, *episkopis* describes somebody who looks at something intently and closely.

In the Greek world, the title *episkopis* was given not to clergy, but to military leaders. It was the term used for the officer from headquarters who would visit the outpost or the training camp to review the troops. The *episkopis* would look carefully through the ranks before giving an evaluation of the combat-readiness of the army. His evaluation would include praise if there was perceived precision among the troops, but also judgment or criticism if he detected weaknesses, sluggishness or sloppiness among them.

From that military environment, the New Testament church took over the term *episkopis* and used it to define someone whose responsibility was to look over the people of God. He was to undertake a careful review, to see how they were doing, to examine the state of their souls. He was an overseer, because his task was to watch over the people of God.

Think back to when you were a child and your parents tried to teach you how to pray. What was the simplest prayer that you uttered? I listen to my grandchildren pray and their prayers are not particularly eloquent. They are very simple, unoriginal, uninspired. They go something like this: 'Dear God, please watch over Mommy and Daddy, and my sister and my dog and cat and my grandfather and grandmother and my teacher.' Notice the phrase that the child uses: 'Watch over'. Little children crave for someone to watch over them, to be on guard, to take care of them.

I remember my experience as a seventeen year old at my father's funeral. The family came to me and said, 'You have to be the man of the house.' Therefore at the funeral parlour when the people came, I stood next to my mother and I gave her my physical support, letting her cry on my shoulder.

During the funeral service, the minister engaged in an eulogy about my father. As he went over my father's personal idiosyncrasies, he made mention of the fact that when he was in his study on the second floor of the church at night-time, and he heard footsteps coming down the hall, he instantly recognised those footsteps as belonging to Bob Sproul, my father.

The moment he made mention of that fact, my mother broke into uncontrollable tears. I tried to comfort her, but I was completely mystified by the reference. When we came home from the cemetery, I asked my mother why she had been particularly affected by what the minister had said. She looked at me, again her eyes misted over, and she said, 'Don't you know what he is talking about? There was something about the way your father walked. I knew when he was in the other room if he was walking across the floor.'

For seventeen years I had known my father and I had not noticed anything unusual about how he walked. He didn't limp, there wasn't anything peculiar. But this pastor, by calling attention to that minor detail indicated to me that, even though he had a congregation of three thousand people, he took the trouble to get to know his flock. He knew each one by name, by face, and even by these tiny idiosyncrasies that defined their personality.

That's what a bishop is supposed to do. A bishop is one who is called upon to know us intimately. Now that can be good news or bad news.

One of the most provocative works ever written in the realm of philosophy was by the French philosopher, Jean-Paul Sartre. It is called *Being and Nothingness*. In this book, Sartre launches into a lengthy argument against the existence of God.

As I thought about the difference between Sartre's and David's responses to the gaze of God, I decided that the tragedy of Sartre was that he had never experienced the benevolent gaze of God, the gracious glance of God.

What made Sartre bristle about the idea of God, was

that he couldn't abide the concept of a cosmic, all-knowing God who could look down from heaven and keep us beneath his gaze every second of our existence. Sartre protested against that by saying, 'Beneath the gaze of God man is reduced into an impersonal object, like a monkey in the zoo, or a painting hanging on the wall. It takes away my freedom; it takes away my personality.'

As I read those lines in Sartre, I had ambivalent feelings. On the one hand I could appreciate how scary it is for any human being to contemplate the idea that somebody somewhere is looking at us every second. Think of the horror in the image of Big Brother in Orwell's *1984*. There is nowhere where one can escape from the Watchman's gaze.

Sometimes, I would just as soon God never put his eyes upon me because, like Adam and Eve in the garden, before the gaze of God I am naked and am ashamed of what I am. But yet there is a part of me that longs desperately to be known intimately by God. I feel like David who, although he was a man after God's own heart, would say, 'Search me, O God, and know my heart; test me and know my anxious thoughts. See if there is any offensive way in me, and lead me in the way everlasting' (Psalm 139:23,24). And then he would ask God to cleanse him.

As I thought about the difference between Sartre's and David's responses to the gaze of God, I decided that the tragedy of Sartre was that he had never experienced the benevolent gaze of God, the gracious glance of God. That occurs when God looks at us, not to judge or destroy us, but to comfort and redeem us.

When I was a teenager, one of the great Hollywood epics was the film version of the Lew Wallace classic, *Ben Hur*. It is about a charioteer who lived during the days of Jesus. When Ben Hur was in slavery to the Romans, he was led in captivity into one of the little villages in Palestine. Because of the scorching sun in the desert he was parched, desperately thirsty. He was helpless in chains, on the ground near a well, but unable to secure any refreshment. Somebody came to the well, took the ladle, dipped it into the water and offered the refreshing water to the thirsty slave.

It was obvious from the story line that the person who gave the drink of water to Ben Hur was Jesus. But in the film, Jesus' face wasn't seen, it wasn't displayed on the screen. All that we saw was Ben Hur crouched in the sand, when suddenly across his own vision came the shadow of a man.

The camera focused on Ben Hur as he looked up, and beheld the face of the one who was helping him. It was the transformed expression of Ben Hur's radiance which communicated to everyone in the theatre that he just looked into the face of Christ. What I came away with from that experience was not so much the thought that Ben Hur looked into the face of Christ, but that Christ stopped to look at Ben Hur.

The message of the Bible is that, despite all the cosmic complexities which require the enormous power and knowledge of a Creator to orchestrate, the God of heaven and earth has an eye upon the sparrow and an eye upon you and upon me.

If we take the word *skopis*, which is a noun and turn to its active verbal form, *skope*, the meaning in Greek changes from 'to look at' into 'to visit'.

Throughout the history of the Jewish people, their prophets promised the people, who often considered themselves desolate and forsaken, that one day there would be 'the Day of Visitation'. It would be the day when their covenant Lord would not only notice his people, nor look at them intensely from heaven, but would descend from heaven and come among them for a personal visit.

This hope and promise was known as the Consolation of Israel. In moments of trial, pain, affliction and suffering, the people would console each other with the promise that some day God would come into their midst.

Luke records an incident when the archangel Gabriel was sent to Palestine, not on this occasion to visit Mary and Joseph, but to visit a priest serving in the temple. The priest was Zechariah, the husband of Elizabeth.

Gabriel informed him that his wife would have a child, and that the child would be named John. John was going to be the forerunner of the Messiah himself. When John was born, Luke tells us that the Holy Spirit came upon Zechariah and he sang a song of praise and thanksgiving. In the song he made mention of the fact that the Lord had visited his people (Luke 1:68). The incarnation, Christ's entrance into this world was, in biblical terms, God *bishoping* or *visiting* his own people.

Peter writes, in his first letter, in reference to Jesus:

'To this you were called, because Christ suffered for you, leaving you an example, that you should follow in his steps. "He committed no sin, and no deceit was found in his mouth." When they hurled their insults at him, he did not retaliate; when he suffered, he made no threats. Instead, he entrusted himself to him who judges justly. He himself bore our sins in his body on the tree, so that we might die to sins and live for righteousness; by his wounds you have been healed. For you were like sheep going astray, but now you have returned to the Shepherd and Overseer (or Bishop) of your souls' (1 Peter 2:21-25).

What a beautiful combination of images! The Good Shepherd who watches over his flock, who knows every sheep that is his. He knows the footfall of each individual sheep, because not only is he the Good Shepherd, but he is the Archbishop of our souls. He doesn't just look; he visits. In his looking and in his visiting, he cares for his people.

part two

Jesus

What did he do?

7

The Need for an Atonement

Just as man is destined to die once, and after that to face judgment, so Christ was sacrificed once to take away the sins of many people; and he will appear a second time, not to bear sin, but to bring salvation to those who are waiting for him (Hebrews 9:27-28).

ONE OF THE MOST IMPORTANT SUBDIVISIONS OF THEOLOGY IS Christology, which is a study of the person and work of Christ. When we consider the crux of the matter of the work of Christ, we go immediately to the cross. The meaning of the cross is the very centre of biblical Christianity.

Symbol of Christianity

I am fascinated by the information that is put out by executives involved in the advertising business. It seems that the whole business of advertising is becoming more and more sophisticated. Billions of dollars are spent creating logos, images, pictures or symbols that instantly communicate a brand or a product.

The universal symbol of Christianity is the cross, because the cross, in a sense, crystallises the

> The universal symbol of Christianity is the cross, because the cross, in a sense, crystallises the essence of the ministry of Jesus.

essence of the ministry of Jesus. Paul, the apostle, said that he was determined to preach nothing except Christ and him crucified (1 Corinthians 2:2). It is not far from the truth to say that all of Paul's writings are an attempt to explain the meaning and significance of that central moment in the life of Christ. Jesus was born and baptised for that event. Indeed, he had been preordained for it. Everything in the life of Jesus converges in that point of climax in his death.

If we were able to read the New Testament as the first generation of people did, it would be crystal-clear to us that the cross of Jesus is at the very core of the preaching, teaching and catechising of the New Testament community. Of course, there is its attending capstone, the resurrection of Jesus and subsequently his ascension to heaven.

Since the cross is of central importance to biblical Christianity, it is essential that Christians have some understanding of its meaning. That would be true in any generation, but it is particularly necessary in this generation. I doubt if there has ever been a period in the 2,000 years of church history, when the significance of the cross, and indeed the necessity of the cross, have been such controversial matters. Never before in Christian history has the need for atonement been so widely challenged as it is being challenged today.

Most people see no need for an atonement
Many people today say that they are not Christians, not because they have never been persuaded of the *truth* of the claims of Christianity, but because they have never

been persuaded of the *need* for what the Bible is teaching.

In most bookshops there are shelves stacked with books on business, sports, self-improvement, sex and marriage, children's stories, as well as fiction. Usually the section on religion is at the back of the shop, and even then the material normally is not orthodox Christianity. The reason shop owners don't have Christian books for sale is because there is not a demand for them from the public. Even in Christian bookshops, there is evidence that people are not seeking in-depth understanding of something as central as the atonement of Christ.

---

*Never before in Christian history has the
need for atonement been so widely
challenged as it is being challenged today.*

If people understood that there is a holy God and that sin is an offence against him, then they would be asking, What must I do to be saved?

Different views of the atonement
I have a theologian friend who frequently makes this statement: 'There are in church history only three basic types of theology: Pelagianism, Semi-pelagianism and Augustinianism. Virtually every church has fallen into one of those three categories.'

Pelagianism is, at best, sub-Christian, and at worst, anti-Christian. The name comes from a fourth century monk,

Pelagius. He was convinced that, although sin is a serious matter in which all people participate, man is basically good and has the ability, even after the Fall of Adam, to live a perfectly righteous and moral life.

In other words, Pelagius believed that man does not need grace in order to be redeemed. Grace does help man live up to the demands of the law, and is there as a remedy for those who are weak and require it, but the possibility exists of fallen man achieving perfect obedience to the law.

Although the church condemned Pelagius and sided with his opponent in the debate, the Church Father, Augustine, the issue has returned in various and sometimes more subtle forms. Aspects of his teaching appear in the Socinianism of the 16th and 17th centuries, and the Liberalism of today. Pelagianism is essentially non-Christian because, at its heart, it is a denial of the atonement of Jesus Christ, a denial of the cross.

Socinianism claimed that Christ became divine after the resurrection. The cross itself was viewed as unconnected to forgiveness. Forgiveness rather stemmed from good works. This system, while not denying miracles, did deny original sin. This heresy laid the groundwork for later Unitarian movements.

Liberalism grew up in the nineteenth century. As a system it denied the authority of Scripture, miracles, original sin, and of course the atonement. It continues today in many mainline denominations.

Pelagians, Socinians and Liberals do have a view of the significance of the cross of Christ. Generally they see

Jesus dying as a moral example, as one who brings inspiration by his commitment and self-sacrifice for humanistic concerns. But they see no need for an atonement.

When I was in the homiletics class in seminary, one of my classmates had to preach on the cross. He preached on the cross as the place where Christ was the lamb slain for us. When he was finished, the professor was furious and verbally attacked the student who was still standing in the pulpit. He angrily said, 'How dare you preach a substitutionary view of the atonement in this day and age!' In his estimation such a view was archaic and old-fashioned.

In Pelagianism there is no need of salvation, therefore Jesus is not a saviour from sin and no atonement was required by God. Semi-pelagianism (or Arminianism) and Augustinianism (also called Calvinism or Reformed), however, represent legitimate differences of biblical interpretation within the Christian family.

Semi-Pelagianism represents an attempt to produce a middle ground position between Pelagianism and Augustinianism. On this view, the Fall has affected man significantly and so without grace he cannot be saved. But the grace that is offered, is offered to people who, despite being seriously weakened by sin, are capable of responding to the offer of the gospel.

The following analogy illustrates this view: fallen man is so overcome by the power of sin, that he is like a person on his deathbed, who has no physical power left to save himself. If he is going to be healed he can't possibly do it through his own strength. The only way he can be made well would be if the physician gave him the medicine that is necessary to restore him. But the man is so desperately ill that he doesn't even have the power to reach out and take the medicine for himself. So the nurse approaches his bed, opens the bottle of medicine, pours it into a spoon, and then moves it over to the dying man's lips. But he must, by his own power, his own will and his own initiative, open his mouth to receive the medicine.

The idea is not that man is still good enough to work his way into the kingdom of God through his own merits, he can't possibly get there without grace. The grace of God is as necessary, according to Arminianism, for salvation, as medicine is to heal this dying man. But a type of cooperation must take place between the patient and the physician for the healing medicine to have its effect. What happens is that God provides the medicine and he brings it to the dying man, but the dying man must cooperate by opening his mouth to receive it.

Here we see the difference between Arminianism and Reformed theology. The Reformed view would be that man is not only critically ill, he is dead. The man doesn't even have the power to open his mouth to receive the healing medicine. Rather, the medicine has to be injected into him by the physician. In other words, as well as providing salvation through Christ, God has to enable the sinner to believe in Christ in order to receive the benefits of salvation.

It is this third view — the Reformed — which I am persuaded is both the biblical view and the orthodox Christian view. An atonement was not merely hypothetically necessary for man's redemption, but was absolutely necessary if a single person was ever going to be reconciled to God.

Why is an atonement necessary?
The heart of the issue has to do with our understanding of the nature of sin and of the character of God. If we are defective in understanding sin and the character of God, it is inevitable that we will come to the conclusion that an atonement is not necessary.

There are three things about the nature of sin that can be said from a biblical perspective.

Firstly, human sin is a *debt*, a failure to do what we are obligated to do. God has given men and women responsibilities for which he holds them accountable. If they do not carry out these responsibilities, they incur a debt in terms of obligation.

Secondly, sin is regarded as an expression of *enmity*, a violation of the personal relationship human beings were supposed to have with their Creator. When they sinned against God they broke a relationship.

Thirdly, sin is regarded as breaking the law of God. In this sense, sin is defined as a *crime*.

It is important that we keep these three concepts clear in our minds in order to see what has to be done to restore the relationship between God and fallen humanity.

If a crime has been committed, then there are *penal sanctions*.

If a debt has been incurred, then there is a *pecuniary sanction*.

Enmity has to do with *personal relationships*. Something serious has happened which needs to be healed. If I steal a thousand dollars from a man I may not *feel* the need to be reconciled to him, but I need it nonetheless! I may not *feel* that I have committed a crime, but I have. I may not *feel* that I have been hostile, but he does not feel particularly loved by my act of theft against him.

Because God is holy, these three elements of sin must be dealt with. God in his purity cannot merely overlook sin. Even in his mercy, the debt, the enmity, the violation must be dealt with.

It is these three aspects of sin: debt, enmity, violation of God's law — and how they relate to the atonement which we come to in the next chapter.

8

Sin and Redemption

What shall we conclude then? Are we any better? Not at all!
We have already made the charge that Jews and Gentiles alike
are all under sin. As it is written:

> 'There is no-one righteous, not even one;
>> there is no-one who understands,
>> no-one who seeks God.
> All have turned away,
>> they have together become worthless;
> there is no-one who does good,
>> not even one.'
> 'Their throats are open graves;
>> their tongues practise deceit.'
> 'The poison of vipers is on their lips.'
>> 'Their mouths are full of cursing and bitterness.'
> 'Their feet are swift to shed blood;
>> ruin and misery mark their ways,
> and the way of peace they do not know.'
>> 'There is no fear of God before their eyes.'

Now we know that whatever the law says, it says to those who
are under the law, so that every mouth may be silenced and the
whole world held accountable to God. Therefore no-one will
be declared righteous in his sight by observing the law; rather,
through the law we become conscious of sin (Romans 3:9-20)

Sin as a debt

WHEN IT IS SAID THAT MAN INCURS A DEBT BY VIRTUE of committing sin, we have to understand the role of God as sovereign over the universe. Whenever we speak of God's sovereignty, we are discussing his authority. Notice that the word 'authority' has another word within it, 'author'. As the author of all things God has authority over all that he creates. His sovereignty means that he has the right to impose obligations.

In our culture there is much confusion over the nature of authority. When people talk about duly constituted authority they are referring to any person or office having the right to impose obligation. If I am under someone's authority, that person has the right to impose an obligation which I am responsible to carry out. If I fail to carry out that obligation, then I face punitive sanctions.

Now God has the authority to impose obligations on his creatures, and he does this by demanding our obedience. God does not rule by referendum, nor does he simply make suggestions or recommendations. He gives commandments. When we fail to perform God-imposed obligations, we incur debt. God is the creditor.

The indebtedness that we have cannot be paid back on an instalment plan. Why? Because of the obligation that God imposes upon his creatures to be sinless or perfect. If I sin once, what must I do to be perfect? How much payment can I make in order to make up for the blemish? I cannot do it. It is impossible.

In our culture we give offenders a second chance. Some actually imagine that everybody *deserves* a second chance. But does justice require that everybody gets a second chance? A second chance involves grace and mercy which are never deserved. So it is nonsense to say that everyone deserves a second chance.

But even if that hypothetical principle were true, what good would it do us? We have long ago used up any second chance. We are not almost impeccable creatures with one tiny little blemish marring a perfect record. Rather the Scriptures describe us as woefully inadequate in terms of our obedience to God. We have incurred a debt that we cannot pay.

What do you suppose is the role of Christ regarding our indebtedness to God? He functions as our *surety*. Surety, just as debt, is an economic term, referring to who guarantees that a debt should be paid. Christ, as our surety, took upon himself to meet the requirement of what must be paid.

Sin as enmity
The reason for our disobedience to God is that we have an inborn hostility towards him. The Bible says that we are by nature enemies of God. We have a natural antipathy in our fallenness towards the reign of God over us.

God is the injured or offended party. God has not manifested enmity towards us, we have violated him. God has never broken a promise; he has never violated a covenant; he has never sworn a vow to us that he failed to pay; he has never treated a human being in this whole world unjustly. We have violated him.

The reason for our disobedience to God is that we have an inborn hostility towards him

---

Yet there are people who are deeply angry with God, because they feel that somehow God has not given them a fair deal. 'How could God allow this to happen to me?' is the complaint. The unspoken statement is that if God was really good and just, he would recognise my merit and treat me accordingly.

But we have to understand that, from a biblical perspective, it is God who is the injured party. I can never say to God that I suffer unjustly.

I may suffer unjustly at human hands. There is a lot of injustice in this world: people lie to one another, cheat one another and harm one another.

On a horizontal level there are all kinds of injustices and the Christian community is called to work for the promotion of justice. But God is never unjust.

When a man violates me and makes me a victim of his unjust activities, I can say to God, 'God, avenge me, vindicate me, restore me, redeem me from this man's unjust activity.'

But I cannot blame God for allowing the man to commit an injustice against me. There is nothing that could ever happen to me in this world which could give me a just reason to assault the integrity of God.

Christ plays in our redemption the role of Mediator. What does a mediator do? He stands in the middle, which is not a very popular place to be because in human elements of estrangement, the mediator usually catches flak from both sides.

Mediation, therefore, in biblical terms includes reconciliation. What does reconciliation presuppose? A prior relationship. What has to happen to that prior relationship before there is a need for reconciliation? It has to be ruptured, there has to be an estrangement of sorts. And the Scriptures speak of the broken relationship between God and man.

In this broken relationship, who is estranged? Obviously man is estranged from God. Men reveal their enmity by continual disobedience. But is it correct to say that God is estranged from man? Is God angry with sinners?

The Bible speaks continually of the wrath of God:

> The wrath of God is being revealed from heaven
> against all the godlessness and wickedness of

men who suppress the truth by their wickedness (Romans 1:18).

What if God, choosing to show his wrath and make his power known, bore with great patience the objects of his wrath — prepared for destruction? (Romans 9:22).

Because of these, the wrath of God is coming (Colossians 3:6).

For God did not appoint us to suffer wrath but to receive salvation through our Lord Jesus Christ (1 Thessalonians 5:9).

True, there is a sense in which the biblical writers were using human language to describe God. But the point is that God is sorely displeased with man's offence. God, being the injured party, is angry with our sin.

One of the distortions of the biblical doctrine of the atonement is this: God the Father is angry with man for his sin, but God the Son because of his love, patience and long-suffering acts as our mediator to calm down the Father who is angry.

But such a view creates a tension within the Godhead itself, as if the Father had one agenda, but the Son persuades him to change his mind. The Father is angry and intends to punish everybody and send them to hell. But the Son says, 'Punish me instead. Let me stand in their place. Let me not only mediate the discussion but let me absorb the anger. Pile it on me, not on them.'

That viewpoint is not only a serious interpretation by sophisticated theologians, but a widespread attitude among Christians. Why is it that evangelical Christians tend to have warm love and affection for Jesus, but totally ignore the Father? Maybe there is still this sense that they can relate to Jesus, but it is difficult to relate to the Father because he was the angry one.

Whose idea was it to have a mediator? Did Jesus go to the Father and say, 'I am tired of listening to all your expressions of anger! I am going to go down there, take the heat off of these people and get you calmed down if you will just let me receive your wrath.' No he did not.

> Take away the substitution of Jesus and you take away the grace of God. You take away the very heartbeat of what the Christian faith is all about.

The truth is the opposite: 'For God so loved the world that he *gave* his one and only Son, that whoever believes in him shall not perish but have eternal life' (John 3:16); 'And we have seen and testify that the Father has *sent* his Son to be the Saviour of the world' (1 John 4:14). The Father *sent* the Son; the Father *gave* the Son for our redemption.

Sin as a crime

In this regard God functions as the governor and judge, his own character being the ultimate standard of righteousness and justice. He functions personally as the judge of heaven and earth. Christ, in the drama of the atonement, is not the judge. He is elevated to the role of judge after his ascension, and that is very significant. But in his descension to this world, he comes under judgment, and his role is as priest-victim. He came to be judged.

At the heart of our whole understanding of the atonement is the necessity of distinguishing between two kinds of indebtedness, a pecuniary debt and a penal debt.

If I steal $10,000 from someone, is it enough for me to say, 'Well, I am sorry it happened. Here is the money, and let's just forget it?' No, because I am in penal debt, I have broken the law.

But suppose I had gone to the man and said, 'I am in trouble. Would you loan me $10,000?' The man gives it to me and we have a perfectly legal, ethical arrangement. Then I find out I can't pay the $10,000, so a friend says, 'Don't worry about it. I'll pay the $10,000.' The debt is paid. The only responsibility I have to the lender is to pay the money. That is a pecuniary debt.

But had I stolen the $10,000 from him, and he complained to the police, could my friend then offer to repay the $10,000? Is the man automatically bound to receive that $10,000 and wipe the slate clean? No. Because in addition to the financial dimension, a crime has been committed. A violation of justice has taken place.

As we have seen, God is both the judge and the injured party. In order for there to be forgiveness for me as a sinner, God had to decide that he would accept a substitutionary payment for my debt and crime to be covered. This prior decision of the Father is one of sheer grace.

What God does is to ensure that justice will be done, that the debt will be paid in full. God does not negotiate away his justice. Therefore the fact that my debt is paid and my crime is punished shows that in the cross there is perfect justice and perfect mercy.

Take away the substitution of Jesus and you take away the grace of God. You take away the very heartbeat of what the Christian faith is all about.

9

Christ our Ransom

For even the Son of Man did not come to be served, but to serve, and to give his life as a ransom for many (Mark 10:45).

THERE MUST HAVE BEEN TIMES IN JESUS' LIFE, PARTICULARLY towards the close of his earthly ministry, when he was disappointed by the failure of his disciples to understand that he was going to Jerusalem to die. Somehow it just didn't get across to them.

On one occasion, just after Jesus had outlined what was going to happen to him in Jerusalem, James and John asked if they could sit on his right and left hands in his kingdom. The angry response of the other disciples showed that they too were thinking the same way (Mark 10:32-41).

Jesus was preparing to enter into his grand passion, and his closest friends were already arguing about the inheritance. But it was in this context that Jesus said something very significant for our understanding of the atonement:

'Jesus called them together and said, "You know that those who are regarded as rulers of the Gentiles lord

it over them, and their high officials exercise authority over them. Not so with you. Instead, whoever
wants to become great among you must be your
servant, and whoever wants to be first must be slave
of all. For even the Son of Man did not come to be
served, but to serve, and to give his life as a ransom
for many" ' (Mark 10:42-45).

Jesus states most succinctly and poignantly that he
came to give his life as a *ransom* for many.

The Greek word *lutron* that is translated 'ransom' here,
is rarely translated in this way. When students begin learn-
ing New Testament Greek, the verb *luo,* which means 'to
loose', is usually in the very first vocabulary list to be
learned. The thrust of the word is 'to set free, to unbind'.
The biblical view of ransom is built upon the idea of setting something free which is being held in captivity. This
understanding of ransom is the root concept behind the
term 'redemption'. In biblical language, a redeemer is
one who provides a ransom.

In the ancient world, the idea of ransom functioned
very similarly to the idea of ransom in our own culture.
We think of ransom in connection with kidnapping where
somebody captures a person and then demands a mon-
etary payment for the free release of the hostage. The word
was also used with reference to a price paid to release a
slave from bondage.

Who fixed the price for the ransom? Not some com-
mittee working out the market rate! The price tag for the

ransom was set by the slaveholder or the kidnapper. Then it was up to the person trying to free the hostage or the slave to assess whether he attached enough value to the person in order to pay the ransom.

This is an important point. In church history there have been various theories about the atonement. Part of the reason is that the atonement, in terms of biblical language imagery, is a multifaceted event.

To whom was the ransom paid?

One of the theories was that, in the transaction of the cross, Jesus paid a ransom to Satan. This view states that Satan had fallen man under bondage in chains. He is a kidnapper who snatched mankind away from God but Christ came and paid the ransom to set them free.

Undoubtedly, an important element of the atonement is the aspect of Christ's work by which he achieved a cosmic victory over Satan, and we musn't minimise in any way that very strong victory motif.

That titanic struggle went on from the very beginning of Jesus' ministry. After his baptism in the River Jordan, the Spirit led him into the wilderness to be tempted by Satan. And when Jesus withstood these temptations, Satan departed from him for a season, a strategic withdrawal, until he could find a better occasion to launch another assault. The conflict went on throughout the ministry of Jesus until, in his death, he conquered Satan.

But this does not mean that the ransom was paid to Satan. After all, if Christ paid a ransom to Satan, who was the victor? If the ransom was paid to Satan, he was the victor. When the Bible speaks of a ransom, it was paid, not to the devil, but to the one who was the offended party in the whole process of sin. Who is that? It is God. Jesus, as the Servant of God, offered himself in payment to God for us.

We cannot get away from the fact that in the biblical concept of ransom we are dealing with two indisputable elements. One is substitution, the other is satisfaction. The New Testament writers understood Jesus' ministry on the cross in terms of him being the substitute, on behalf of others, paying a ransom (satisfaction for sin).

Karl Barth often said that the single most important Greek word in the New Testament is the little word *huper*. It means 'on behalf of'. It illustrates the recurring refrain of Jesus' own self-understanding: I am doing this, not for myself, but for others.

The cross and the wrath of God

Two important terms which are used in explaining the atonement are 'propitiation' and 'expiation'. The way to remember the difference is to understand the prefixes: *ex* usually means 'away from' or 'out of'; *pro* usually means 'for'.

The word *expiation* means to remove something, to take it away; in biblical terms it has to do with taking away guilt by paying a ransom or offering an atonement. The act of expiation removes the problem by paying for it, by a penalty, a ransom, or a sacrifice.

Propitiation has to do with the object of the expiation.

It has to do with that which brings about a change in God's attitude, whereby sinners are restored into fellowship with him. There is a sense in which we can speak of God's being appeased, of his anger against sinners being removed.

Sometimes the same Greek word is translated both by expiation and propitiation, but there is a slight difference in the terms. Expiation is the completed act which resulted in the change of God's disposition towards us, namely, what Christ did on the cross. The result of Christ's work of expiation is that God is propitiated, and the consequence is that we are reconciled to God. Expiation has to do with the ransom that was paid, and propitiation with the attitude of the one who received the ransom.

> The work of Christ was done to placate the wrath of God.

There is involved in expiation and propitiation an act of placation. The work of Christ was done to placate the wrath of God. This idea of placating the wrath of God has done little to placate the wrath of modern theologians. They become very angry about the idea of placating the wrath of God. They think that it is beneath the dignity of God to be placated, that something has to be done to appease him.

We have to be very careful how we understand the wrath of God, but the concept of placating the wrath of God has to do, not with a peripheral point of theology, but with the essence of salvation.

The word *salvation* in the Bible is used in different ways: it can refer to being rescued from certain defeat in battle or surviving a life-threatening illness. We talk that way in our own language.

Therefore when we talk about salvation, theologically, we have to discover from what ultimately we are saved. Paul, in I Thessalonians 1:10, says that Christ has saved believers from the wrath to come.

We cannot understand the teaching of Jesus apart from this. He constantly warned people that the whole world will yet be judged. What was done in secret will be public. Every word will be brought into the judgment. Jesus preached the crisis of a certain judgment of the world, when God will pour out his wrath against the ungodly and impenitent. The only hope of escape from the wrath of God is to be covered by the atonement of Christ.

The supreme achievement of the cross is that Jesus has placated the wrath of God which would burn against me were I not covered by the sacrifice of Christ. There is no wrath now for believers.

10

Blessing or Curse?

Christ redeemed us from the curse of the law by becoming a curse for us, for it is written: 'Cursed is everyone who is hung on a tree.' He redeemed us in order that the blessing given to Abraham might come to the Gentiles through Christ Jesus, so that by faith we might receive the promise of the Spirit (Galatians 3:13-14).

THE CROSS OF CHRIST IS AN EVENT IN HISTORY OF SUCH OUT-standing importance and significance that it is easy to overlook the fact that the cross was not an isolated historical event. Rather, the atonement of Christ is the climax of centuries of redemptive history. God had set certain things in motion, long before history reached its acme in the death of Christ.

In the Reformed tradition, we understand the atoning work of Christ within the broader framework of what we call the covenant. It is impossible to have a full understanding of the death of Christ apart from an understanding of the covenant that is worked out in the Old and New Testaments.

For example, what was Jesus doing in the Upper Room the night before he was crucified? He wanted to celebrate the Passover with his friends one last time. Jesus made painstaking preparations to meet with them to celebrate the central ceremony and sacrament of the old covenant. While he was in that process, he gave new meaning to the old signs, and instituted a new covenant. With respect to the cup, he said, 'This is the blood of the new covenant which is shed for the remission of sins'. Suddenly the wine no longer refers to the Passover event but to the blood shed by Christ in his atoning death.

The blessings and curses of the covenant

A study of the elements of a covenant in the ancient world reveals that, though the content of covenants may differ from culture to culture, there were certain elements and aspects of a covenant which were virtually universal.

Whenever a legal agreement was entered into, the sovereign one in the covenant would identify himself and give an historical prologue where he would rehearse the history of his relationship to the subordinates in the covenant. When God entered into a covenant with Israel, he identified himself. He said, 'I am the LORD your God, who brought you out of Egypt' (Exodus 20:2).

Then the terms of the covenant, stipulations, would be set forth. All covenants, such as marriage or industrial contracts, have stipulations. In the ancient world every covenant had dual sanctions. These would be the rewards for keeping the terms, and penalties if the terms were violated. In the Old Testament the reward for keeping the covenant was called a *blessing*, and the penalty for violating the covenant was called a *curse*.

In Deuteronomy 28, where part of the terms of the covenant that God made with the people of Israel are spelled out, there are recorded both blessings and curses. In verses 1-14, there is a list of blessings:

BLESSING OR CURSE?

'If you fully obey the LORD your God and carefully follow all his commands that I give you today, the LORD your God will set you high above all the nations on earth. All these blessings will come upon you and accompany you if you obey the LORD your God:

You will be blessed in the city and blessed in the country.

The fruit of your womb will be blessed, and the crops of your land and the young of your livestock – the calves of your herds and the lambs of your flocks.

Your basket and your kneading trough will be blessed.

You will be blessed when you come in and blessed when you go out.

The LORD will grant that the enemies who rise up against you will be defeated before you. They will come at you from one direction but flee from you in seven.

The LORD will send a blessing on your barns and on everything you put your hand to. The LORD your God will bless you in the land he is giving you.

The LORD will establish you as his holy people, as he promised you on oath, if you keep the commands of the LORD your God and walk in his ways. Then all the peoples on earth will see that you are called by the name of the LORD, and they will fear you. The LORD will grant you abundant prosperity – in the fruit of your womb, the young of your livestock and the crops of your ground – in the land he swore to your forefathers to give you.

The LORD will open the heavens, the storehouse of his bounty, to send rain on your land in season and to bless all the work of your hands. You will lend to many nations but will borrow from none. The LORD will make you the head, not the tail. If you pay attention to the commands of the LORD your God that I give you this day and carefully follow them, you will always be at the top, never at the bottom. Do not turn aside from any of the commands I give you today, to the right or to the left, following other gods and serving them.'

But look at verses 15-68: curse after curse.

We need to understand what it means to be blessed and what it means to be cursed.

On one occasion I was in Knoxville for an evaluation meeting of the New King James Bible. During the discussion, one of the things that we had to respond to was the debate in biblical translation over the best way to render into contemporary English the Beatitudes of Jesus. Should it be, '*Blessed* are those who are poor in spirit', or should it be '*Happy* are those who are in poor in spirit'? There were some who wanted to use 'Happy'. I disagreed, because there is a special theological significance to the word 'blessed' which is not conveyed by the English word 'happy'.

To the Jew, blessedness was supreme favour from the

hands of God. A good way of explaining this is to look at the Hebrew benediction: 'The LORD bless you and keep you; the LORD make his face shine upon you and be gracious to you; the LORD turn his face towards you and give you peace' (Numbers 6:24-26).

In this benediction there is a poetic structure and rhythm. This is a form of Hebrew literature called *parallelism*. The first stanza has two parts: the Lord bless you, and, the Lord keep you. The prayer was for two things. How important was it for the Jew to be kept? If ever there was a people who had very little certainty about their future, it was the Jewish people. The idea of being preserved, maintained and sustained for some kind of continuity is very deeply rooted in the Jewish heart.

But in the Hebrew blessing there is also a form of parallelism called *synthetic parallelism*, where every verse means the same thing, only stated in different words to give poetic richness and diversity. If we want to understand how the Jew assessed blessedness, we get a clue from this blessing. It would be when the face of God shone upon them, when God would lift up the light of his countenance upon them. The supreme blessedness to the Jew is what we call the Beatific Vision, the vision of God. To be able to look God in the face.

If we study this carefully in its other replications in the Old Testament, we see that 'blessedness' has to do with the proximity and remoteness of the presence of God. The closer to the immediate presence of God, the greater the blessedness, the further removed from the face of God, the less the blessedness.

A curse is the opposite of blessing. A curse would reverse the blessing and say, 'May the Lord curse you and destroy you! May the Lord turn his back upon you and be judgmental towards you! May the Lord turn off the light of his countenance and leave you in darkness and give you turmoil!' This would be the curse of the covenant, rather than the blessedness of the covenant. When the Jew described the Gentiles, he would say that they were strangers to the covenant, foreign to the household of Israel.

> The supreme blessedness to the Jew is what we call the Beatific Vision, the vision of God. To be able to look God in the face.

But the point to be stressed is that for the Jew to be blessed was to have God draw near. In Psalm 46, when the psalmist sang, 'We will not fear', why did he say so? He refers to the seas roaring and the mountains being carried into the midst of the sea, calamities taking place all around him. But there is a river, the streams whereof make glad the city of God; God is in the midst of her, we shall not be moved. The reason for the confidence of the psalmist was the presence of God.

When the people of Israel encamped in the desert on their journey to Canaan, they were to pitch their tents and arrange their tribes according to a structure that God had given them. The tribes would camp in a circle. What was at the centre? It was the tabernacle. God pitched his tent right in the midst of the people, as if he was saying, 'Here I am.'

Quite clearly, the biblical concept of blessedness was understood in terms of the proximity of the presence of God. Conversely, the curse of the covenant was to be cut off from the presence of God, never to see the light of his countenance, to be cast into the outer darkness.

The curse of the cross
In the third chapter of Galatians, Paul refers to the covenant God made with Abraham which would result in Abraham being a blessing (see Genesis 12). Through him all of the nations of the world would be blessed.

Paul explains that this blessedness was for those who live by faith. All who rely on observing the law, that is trying to achieve a relationship with God by their own good works and their own performance, are still under a curse. Paul was remembering the terms of the covenant: if we don't keep every one of the laws, we are under the curse. He says in verse 11, 'Clearly no-one is justified before God by the law, because "The righteous will live by faith." The law is not based on faith; on the contrary, "The man who does these things will live by them."'

But then Paul says, 'Christ redeemed us from the curse of the law by becoming a curse for us, for it is written, "Cursed is everyone who is hung on a tree." ' Paul states that on the cross Christ became a curse, that all of the sanctions and penalties of the law were borne by him.

In the Old Testament there were negative sanctions imposed for certain situations which were considered sacrilegious, or imposed on a person who had become unclean. When we look closely at the events surrounding the crucifixion of Jesus, we discover some amazing things that occurred which resulted in elements of the Old Testament being fulfilled to the minutest detail.

Jesus indicated that he would be delivered to the Gentiles for judgment. He lived during a time of Roman occupation, when the Romans, though they allowed a certain amount of home rule to their conquered vassals, did not permit them to impose the death penalty. The Jews did not have the authority to put Christ to death. All they could do was to meet in council, deliver Jesus to Pilate, and get Pilate to pronounce sentence.

So Jesus was delivered to the Gentiles who were outside the camp. He was delivered into the hands of the pagans, outside of where the face of God shined, outside of where the light of his countenance fell. And he was delivered into their hands for judgment. The Jews did not execute by crucifixion; they did it by stoning, but the Romans did it by crucifixion. The method of Jesus' death was by hanging upon a tree. The Bible does not say, 'Cursed is everyone who is stoned', but 'Cursed is everyone who hangs upon a tree'.

Another detail has to with the actual site of the execution, which was outside Jerusalem. Once Jesus was condemned to be executed, he was physically led out of the city. Like the scapegoat in the Day of Atonement ritual, Jesus was taken outside the Holy City where the presence of God is concentrated. On the day of atonement the sins of the nation were ceremonially transferred to the scapegoat, which was then driven into the wilderness, into the place of darkness.

When Jesus was put on the cross, an astronomical perturbation occurred in the middle of the afternoon. It became dark, literally. The darkness involved a blotting out of the sun's light, perhaps even an eclipse. In the midst of that darkness, Jesus cried, 'My God, my God, why have you forsaken me?' (Matthew 27:46). It was one of the most pregnant utterances that ever came from the lips of Jesus. There have been all kinds of interpretations of what he meant.

Albert Schweitzer thought it was proof that Jesus died in disillusionment. According to Schweitzer, Jesus had expected God to deliver him, but realised

> God turned his back on his Son. No wonder he screamed! He screamed from the depths of his soul.

that God had let him down in the final moments. So Jesus died as a disappointed hero.

Others have noticed that the words are a quotation from Psalm 22. They say that Jesus was identifying himself with the Suffering Servant of Psalm 22, and is therefore reciting poetry on his deathbed.

Others suggest that Jesus, in his humanity, felt forsaken on the cross, but was not really forsaken.

If Jesus was not truly forsaken on the cross, however,

we are still in our sins. We have no redemption, because the whole point of the cross was that Jesus bore our sins and the sanctions of the covenant.

Circumcision a picture of the curse

What was the sign of the old covenant? It was circumcision. Circumcision had two meanings, one positive and one negative, mirroring the blessing and cursing. The positive was that God was cutting out Israel from the other nations, setting it apart to be a holy nation, to be a blessing. The negative was that if the Jew failed to keep every one of the terms of the covenant, he would be cut off from God's presence, just as his foreskin had been ritually cut off.

The cross is the supreme circumcision, because when Jesus took the curse upon himself, he so identified with the sin of his people that he became a curse. God cut him off and justly so, because at that moment Christ became sin. Jesus, on the cross, was the most grotesque, most obscene mass of sin concentrated in the history of the world. Remember God is too holy even to look at iniquity. Therefore when Christ was hanging on the cross, the Father turned his back and cut off his Son. God forsook him.

I have heard many sermons about the nails and the thorns. Granted the physical agony of crucifixion was a ghastly thing. But thousands of people were crucified, and others have experienced even more horrible, painful, excruciating deaths. But only one has received the full measure of the curse of God. I doubt if Jesus was even aware of the nails and the spear, he was so overwhelmed by the outer darkness.

On the cross Jesus was in hell, totally bereft of the grace and the presence of God, utterly separated from all blessedness of the Father. If you are a Christian, remember Jesus became a curse for you, so that one day you will be able to see the face of God, and have the light of his countenance fall on you.

God turned his back on his Son. No wonder he screamed! He screamed from the depths of his soul.

How long did he have to endure it? A second of it is of infinite value. It is enough. When Jesus said, 'It is finished' (John 19:30), he was not referring to his life or to the pain of the nails. No. He was referring to the darkness being over. The light of God's face again shone upon him and he said, 'Into your hands I commit my spirit' (Luke 23:46).

Every time I read about the cross I am just in awe of what happened.

11

Securing our Faith

I am the good shepherd. The good shepherd lays down his life for the sheep (John 10:11).

On one occasion, my local newspaper carried a story of residents of a town being upset at a waste of taxpayers' money. The previous week, workers had painted new white lines down the centre of the highway. During the following week, another crew put a new asphalt topping over the fresh white lines.

You may wonder what that has to do with the atonement. There has been great controversy in the history of the church concerning the intent of God in the act of the atonement. For whom did Christ die? What was God's design and purpose in the whole dynamic activity of the cross? Some theories function just like those in charge of public roads in the newspaper article.

The issue has focused on the Reformed doctrine called 'limited atonement' or 'particular redemption'. Limited atonement is linked historically to the name of Calvin and Calvinism. It is an integral part of the Five Points of Calvinism. The acrostic TULIP gives the first letter of each of the five distinctive points of Calvinism. The T stands for Total Depravity, U for Unconditional Election,

L for Limited Atonement, I for Irresistible Grace and P for the Perseverance of the Saints. These are the five distinctives of Calvinistic theology.

None of those five points has created more controversy than limited atonement. In fact there are many who call themselves Four-Point Calvinists. They believe in all four points except limited atonement. I have had the opportunity to discuss this view with some of them, and I have discovered, in every single instance except one, that each person was a No-Point Calvinist. They thought they believed in total depravity, unconditional election, irresistible grace and the perseverance of the saints, but they didn't understand them either.

The one exception happened to be a teacher of theology. I was really interested in that. I sat down at a table with him, and said, 'I really want to hear how you handle this because I trust you. I know you are knowledgeable in theology, and I want to hear how you think this through.' I expected, frankly, that he would not have an accurate understanding.

However, to my astonishment he explained total depravity, unconditional election, irresistible grace and perseverance of the saints as clearly as any strict Calvinist ever articulated them. I was rejoicing. But I was also amazed, so I said, 'Tell me about your understanding of limited atonement.' As he gave me his understanding, I found out that he was a Five-Point Calvinist. He believed in limited atonement and didn't know it!

My point is that there is a lot of confusion about what limited atonement means and the controversy in some cases extenuates the confusion.

We have to understand, first of all, that the concept of limited atonement was not introduced by John Calvin, and is not unique to Calvinism. The debate over the extent and the design of the atonement really heated up in the fourth century, and the debate focused on the teaching of Augustine over against Pelagius. Augustine was the first of the early Church Fathers to clearly articulate the concept in a theological way.

Incidentally the thing flared up again in a fierce debate within the Roman Catholic church between the Jesuits who denied the limited atonement, and the Jansenists who rigorously affirmed it.

Let's look at some of the distortions so that we can clear up misconceptions about what Augustine meant.

The acrostic TULIP gives the first letter of each
of the five distinctive points of Calvinism
T stands for Total Depravity,
U for Unconditional Election,
L for Limited Atonement,
I for Irresistible Grace and
P for the Perseverance of the saints

The value of Christ's atoning death
The question has to do, first of all, with the value of the atoning sacrifice of Jesus Christ. Classical Augustinianism teaches that the atonement of Jesus Christ is *sufficient* for

all men. The value of the sacrifice that Christ offered to the Father is of infinite value. There is enough merit in the work of Jesus Christ to cover the sins of every human being who has ever lived. So there is no limit to the value of the sacrifice that is made. In that sense, what Christ did on the cross is sufficient, objectively considered, to cover the sins of every individual in the world. There is no debate about the sufficiency of Christ's atonement.

But there is a distinction between the *sufficiency* of the atonement and the *efficiency* of the atonement. The question really is, Was Jesus' death efficient for everybody? This is where we find all kinds of subtle differences of opinion.

Does the atonement result in saving everybody automatically? Does Christ's death on the cross have the effect of saving the whole world? There are people who believe that Jesus died for the whole world in the sense that his death on the cross brought about that result. Such people are Universalists. Now Arminians do not believe in limited atonement, but neither are they Universalists. Calvinists and Arminians agree that not everybody is saved through the atoning death of Jesus Christ. So there is, in some sense, a limit to the efficiency of the cross.

The real issue is the question of the intent and of the design. Arminianism teaches that God, when he planned the way of salvation, intended the atonement for all men, and designed it as such. Calvinism says that God designed the atonement of Jesus Christ to be for the elect only. Every single person for whom Christ died is saved.

The Calvinistic view is not that God saw the human

race plunged into trouble and, after sending the Saviour, hopes that some will respond to his grace. No, he sent a Saviour designed to save and his will is not frustrated at that point. Jesus did not bear the sins of the world with the hope that maybe somebody would be saved. He went with the certain knowledge that his sacrifice on the cross would in fact save people.

The work on the cross is the most significant part of the priestly work of Jesus Christ. The High Priestly prayer of Jesus, recorded in John 17, is astonishing at one point. He says in verses 6 and 7: 'I have revealed you to those whom you gave me out of the world. They were yours; you gave them to me and they have obeyed your word. Now they know that everything you have given me comes from you.'

Then he says, 'I pray for them. I am not praying for the world, but for those you have given me, for they are yours' (verse 9). Jesus, in the most poignant prayer of intercession he ever offered in this world, makes it explicit that he is not praying for everybody in the world. He is praying for the elect.

Is it conceivable to you that Jesus would be willing to die for the whole world but not pray for the whole world? It just doesn't make sense. Jesus came to lay down his life for his sheep, to die for his people (John 10:11). His atonement would be effective in the case of those for whom he intended it to be effective.

There is another problem with these alternative views. If an atonement is made that removes my sin, what else could possibly be necessary for salvation? If your sins are atoned for, you are saved whether you want it or not. This was the issue earlier in this century with the theology of Karl Barth. People objected to Barth's theology on the grounds that he was a Universalist, but Barth insisted to the day he died that he was misunderstood, that he was not a Universalist.

Barth believed that in the cross we see God's 'Yes' to all mankind. But Barth also believed that men can say no to the cross and refuse this work that God has done for all men. God's 'yes' is for the whole world, but men can still say 'no'. And in fact they do say no. However, God's 'yes' overrules man's 'no'. But if God's 'yes' overrules man's 'no' then surely the universal overrules the particular and there is good reason for people to interpret Barth's theology as being universalistic?

Some may object, Why does the Bible say that he died for the whole world? The key lies in understanding the usage of the word 'world' in the Bible. The point that the New Testament is making, particularly to a Jewish audience, is that Jesus is not only the Saviour of Jewish people. People from every race are numbered among the elect. The atonement has implications for the whole world, but that doesn't mean each and every person in the world.

There is a universal effect of the cross, in the sense that everybody benefits from the death of Christ, although not in the full sense of being saved by it. Let me just give you one example of that. Through the death of Christ the church is born, the gospel is preached and wherever the gospel is preached, there is an increase in virtue and righteousness in the society where people adopt it. People have benefited from the church's commitment to hospitals, to orphanages, and so on where the benefits are not restricted simply to Christians.

Universal offer

Calvinists believe that the atonement of Jesus Christ is to be offered to all men. In this they are biblical. They are to proclaim the gospel to all men, and say that God so loved the world that he gave his Son that whoever believes in him shall not perish but have eternal life (John 3:6). But some people think that limited atonement casts a shadow over the universal offer and that a real Calvinist will have no passion for evangelism.

Calvinists offer the gospel to all men, knowing full well that not everybody will respond to it. But they also know without a shadow of a doubt that some definitely will respond to the gospel. The Arminian doesn't know that. The Arminian can only hope that somebody will be persuaded to co-operate with grace and take advantage of the benefits offered in the atonement.

The doctrine of limited atonement means that God intended and designed the way of salvation for his people. The Arminian believes that there was an expiation of sin, but it is conditional. The condition that must be met is *faith*. But from their point of view, all there is is a potential expiation and a potential propitiation. There is a very real sense where the atonement itself is dependent upon human response. And that is what Augustine found so repugnant.

Most people react against the idea of a Limited Atonement because it seems to take away from the greatness of the work of Christ. The very opposite is the case. It is the Arminian position which diminishes and devalues the full impact and power of the atonement of Jesus Christ. The point we are making is that God accomplished what he set out to accomplish, and Christ accomplishes what he sets out to accomplish. God's sovereign will is not at the mercy of our personal and individual response to it. Otherwise you have the theoretical possibility that God goes to all this trouble to save the world, and potentially nobody is saved.

One of the sweetest statements from the lips of Jesus in the New Testament is when he says, 'Come, you who are blessed by my Father; take your inheritance, the kingdom prepared for you since the creation of the world' (Matthew 25:34). Salvation was not an attempt to correct a mistake in the mind of God. From all eternity, God had determined to redeem his people, and what he determined to do has in fact been accomplished in the work of Jesus Christ.

12

Justification by Faith

Therefore, since we have been justified through faith, we have peace with God through our Lord Jesus Christ, through whom we have gained access by faith into this grace in which we now stand. And we rejoice in the hope of the glory of God (Romans 5:1-2).

AT THE TIME OF THE PROTESTANT REFORMATION, MARTIN Luther insisted that the doctrine of justification by faith alone is the article upon which the church stands or falls. In fact, in his much celebrated debate with Erasmus of Amsterdam, Luther thanked Erasmus for debating the real issue and not fooling around with trifles. The issue was: How does the cross of Christ relate to individuals?

In this chapter we turn from studying what happened objectively at the cross, to look at how the benefit of Christ's work is appropriated personally. What relevance does it have for us as individuals that Christ died on the cross?

The theological term for this area of study is *justification*, and it is at the heart of the gospel. Yet there are many people in the church who have trouble defining the very meaning of justification. To understand it we have to go back to basics.

So far in this section of the book, we have seen that the need for an atonement is related to the problem of human sin and to the character of God, particularly his holiness and justice. There is the basic problem: God is just and man is unjust. The fundamental question, therefore, is how are these two parties going to relate?

Man's total depravity

The term used to describe man's condition is *total depravity*. People wince whenever they hear this term because of a confusion in their minds between *total* depravity and *utter* depravity. Utter depravity would mean that man was as bad, as corrupt, as he possibly could be. And there is probably no human being in this world, right now, who is utterly corrupt. But this is so only by the restraining power of God's common grace.

Total depravity does not mean that men are as bad as they conceivably could be, because it is possible for all of us to commit either more gross and heinous sins or numerically more frequent sins.

When the Protestant Reformers used the term 'total depravity', they meant that sin in its power, influence, inclination, affects the whole man. Our bodies are fallen, our hearts are fallen, our minds are fallen. There is no part of us that escapes the ravages of our sinful human nature.

The apostle Paul elaborates on this fallen human condition when he says, 'There is no-one righteous, not even one; there is no-one who understands, no-one who seeks God' (Romans 3:10-11). Now that is a radical statement. Paul says that fallen man never does a single good deed. Yet that seems to contradict our experience, because we see all kinds of people, who are not Christians, perform acts of self-sacrificial heroism, kindness and charity. Calvin called this 'civil righteousness'.

The reason why we have this problem is because when the Bible describes goodness it does so from two distinct perspectives.

First of all, there is the measuring rod of the law which assesses the external performance of human beings. For example, God says men are not allowed to steal, and so if you live your whole life without stealing, it could be said that you have a good record. The law has been kept externally.

But, in addition to the external measuring rod, there is also the consideration of the heart, the internal motivation for our behaviour.

God told Samuel that man judges by outward appearance whereas God looks at the heart (1 Samuel 16:7). From a biblical perspective, to do a good deed in the fullest sense of the word requires not only that the deed conforms outwardly to the standards of God's law, but that it proceeds from a heart that loves God and wants to honour him.

Remember the commandment: 'Love the Lord your God with all your heart' (Matthew 22:37). Is there anybody reading this book who has loved God with all of his heart for the last five minutes? No. Nobody has loved God with all of his heart since he got out of his bed this morning. Add to that the remainder of the verse, '... and with all your soul and with all of your mind'.

How many times I have been lazy and slothful and too

bored to apply myself in the fullest possible measure to know God! I have not loved God with all of my mind. If I loved God with all of my mind, there would never be another thought in my head.

When we consider human performance from this total perspective, we can see why Paul came to the apparently radical conclusion that there are none who do good. There is no goodness in the full sense of the word found among men. This implies that even our finest activities are tainted with sin.

I have never performed an act of charity, sacrifice or heroism out of a heart that loved God completely. Externally, all kinds of virtuous acts are going on, both among believers and unbelievers. But God takes the inner attitudes and motives into account as well.

On the other hand, God is too holy even to look at iniquity. God is perfectly just. How can an unjust person stand in the presence of God? Which means, how can the unjust person be made just? He cannot start over again or erase the past. Once a person sins it is impossible for him ever to be perfect, because he has already lost his perfection by his initial sin.

Some may say that there is not really a problem because God can overlook sin. For the sake of argument, let's imagine that God could overlook sin. This would mean that God gives sinners eternal life by sacrificing his justice.

This is where, as we have seen, Christ comes to act as our mediator. When we consider our redemption, we tend to think that salvation comes to us through the death of

Christ. In doing so, it is very easy to overlook something of crucial significance.

If I ask a child, 'What did Jesus do for you?', he will say, 'Jesus died for my sins.' But if that is all Jesus did, why didn't he just come down from heaven and go straight to the cross? The point of the atonement is that a *just* man died for the unjust. Jesus had to first live *a life of obedience* before his death could mean anything. He had to acquire merit at the bar of justice. What is often overlooked in justification is that a double transaction takes place.

The life of Jesus
How many blemishes were there in the life of Jesus?

John the Baptist described Jesus as 'the Lamb of God who takes away the sin of the world' (John 1:29). He was alluding to the Old Testament ritual which involved the sacrifice of a lamb which had no defect. John was saying that Jesus was sinless.

On another occasion, Jesus himself said to the Pharisees, 'Can any of you prove me guilty of sin?' (John 8:46). In a sense we become anaesthetised by our familiarity with the New Testament stories and so sometimes when Jesus makes a radical statement, we don't even blink!

What would you think if I said to you, 'You think I'm a sinner? Name one of my sins.' You might have difficulty doing that if you did not know me. But what if I went to my home town and said, 'Name one of my sins?'

Well, here was Jesus in his home town, surrounded by

people who knew him, and yet he challenges them to find a sin in his life. No wonder they picked up rocks and started to attack him.

Jesus knew he had no sin. His meat and his drink was to do the will of the Father. Zeal for his Father's house consumed him. He was a man whose passion in life was obedience to God.

So now we have this situation: one unjust party — sinful men and women — and two just parties — a just God and now a just Mediator, Jesus Christ, who is altogether holy.

Imputation of Christ's righteousness

A biblical imagery of the atonement is *imputation*. The justification of which the New Testament speaks is called, in the Protestant tradition, *forensic justification*. Forensics has to do with authoritative, formal acts of declaration. Forensic justification means that a person is declared to be just at the tribunal of God. Justification takes place when the Supreme Judge of heaven and earth pronounces one just.

But the question still remains, On what possible grounds could God justify an unjust person?

In the New Testament we find the image of Jesus as the Lamb of God who takes away the sin of the world. How did he take away the sin of the world?

Earlier we noted that this image was connected to the Old Testament sacrificial system. The priest put his hands on the lamb and symbolically transferred the sins of the people to the animal that was to be sacrificed, or to the scapegoat which was to go out into the wilderness.

Jesus is said to bear our sins. Christ willingly took them upon himself. Once the sin has been imputed to Jesus, God looks at Christ and sees a mass of sinfulness, because of the sin that has been transferred to him.

But if that single transfer was all that happened, we would never be justified. Even if Jesus paid the penalty for all of my sins, I still would not get into the kingdom of God. It would keep me out of hell but I would still not be just. I would have no righteousness of which to speak. Remember it is not simply innocence that gets me into the kingdom of God, it is righteousness.

The point is that there is a double transfer. Not only is the sin of man imputed to Christ, but the righteousness of Christ is imputed to man. So when God declares me just he is not lying.

Incidentally, Roman Catholicism has trouble with this Protestant concept, which it describes as a legal fiction. They recoil from it because they believe that the Protestant view of imputation casts a shadow on the integrity of God because he declares people just who are not just.

The response of the Reformers was that if the imputation were fictional, then when God declared us just it would be a legal fiction. It would be a blemish on the character of God. But the point of the gospel is that the imputation is real. God really laid sins on Christ, and he really transfers the righteousness of Christ to sinners. Those who are in Christ really possess the righteousness of Jesus Christ by imputation. That is why he can be my Saviour. Not merely because he died, but because he lived.

Theologians like to have Latin phrases. One of my favourites was offered by Luther as a very important phrase to capture this concept of imputation. The essence of our salvation is found in the phrase: *Simul iustis et peccatorum* (at the same time, just and sinner). The word *simul* (from which we get the English word 'simultaneous'), means 'at the same time'; *iustis* means 'just'; *et* means 'and'; *peccatorum* means 'sinner'. This is the glory of the doctrine of justification by faith alone: the person who is in Christ is, at the very same instant, just and a sinner.

Justification by faith alone means very simply this: justification is by Christ alone. It is by his merit, his righteousness, his life, his death, that we can stand in the presence of a Holy God.